What People Are Saying About
Finding the Hero in Your Husband . . .

"Psychologist Julianna Slattery blends her deep faith and knowledge of scripture with her personal experience as a wife, mother and counselor to give us an honest and practical book on marriage that inspires wives to strive toward intimacy and godliness."

—**Gigi Graham Tchividjian**
author, *Mothers Together,*
Weatherproof Your Heart and *For Women Only*

"This excellent book in plain English takes marriage very joyfully and the Bible very seriously. It is filled with practical advice about life's difficult passages, but it is also filled with hope. I think Paul would have recommended it."

—**Knute Larson**
senior pastor, The Chapel

FINDING THE HERO IN YOUR HUSBAND

Surrendering the Way God Intended

Julianna Slattery, Psy.D.

Health Communications, Inc.
Deerfield Beach, Florida

www.hci-online.com

Library of Congress Cataloging-in-Publication Data

Slattery, Julianna
    Finding the hero in your husband : surrendering the way God intended / Julianna Slattery.
      p.   cm.
    ISBN 1-55874-930-6 (pbk.)
    1. Wives—Religious life.   2. Christian women—Religious life.
  I. Title

BV4528. 15 .S53 2001
248.8'435—dc21

2001024689

Publisher: Health Communications, Inc.
        3201 S.W. 15th Street
        Deerfield Beach, FL 33442-8190

Cover design by Lawna Patterson Oldfield
Book inside design by Dawn Grove

To Michael

Contents

Acknowledgments ❧

*H*ad it not been for Lisa Baxter and "Taylor," this book may have never been in print. Thank you for the way God has used you to encourage and direct me in this project. Thank you to the Health Communications family. Specifically, I am grateful to Christine Belleris, Allison Janse and Kathleen Fox for your expertise in editing, as well as your patience with me!

Thank you Debbie Prinz, John Rasnic and Julie Anderson for giving of your special talents to make this book possible. So many family and friends read and re-read the manuscripts. Thank you for your encouragement and input: Warren and Cheryl Kniskern, Amy McDougald, Wendy Rybka, Steve and Pam Rybka, Emily Zimmerman, Sue Burnham, Christie Orosz, Anne Volk, Janice Zekoski, and Sara Steigerwald.

Over the past several years, the Lord has given me several mentors who have been critical to encouraging and guiding my vision. Specifically, thank you Dr. Stephan Tchividjian, Dr. Phillip Farber, Dr. Wanda Bethea, and Dr. Michael Misja for the contributions you have made to my thinking and personal development.

The Lord has also blessed me with wonderful parents, Larry and Jo Rybka. Dad, thank you for teaching me about godliness through your love, your integrity and your faithfulness. Thank you for always investing in me, and mostly, for your prayers. You have given me the confidence to develop my dreams and abilities and to trust God with them. Mom, this book is about you. Each day that I lived in your home, I witnessed your daily devotion to finding the hero in Dad. You taught me that intimacy with God would free me to contribute to the leadership of my husband. I cannot thank you enough for what you have taught me about God, about marriage and about life.

Saving the best for last, special thanks to my husband, Michael. It is only through your love and encouragement that I could undertake this adventure. Although you have not physically written these words, you are the co-author. You have contributed so greatly to who I am and all that I do that this is your project as much as mine. I am so honored to be your wife and I look forward to the rest of our journey together. You ready, Lewis?

Foreword

*A*s one who has written on the subject of marriage, divorce and remarriage, there is one extremely powerful and challenging scripture which cuts to my heart as a husband and father: "Husbands, love your wives, just as Christ loved the church and gave himself up for her . . ." (Ephesians 5:25) What an awesome responsibility! How could any man possibly fulfill this vital role—even with God's ever-present power in his life?

Wives yearn to be loved and cherished in ways that seem beyond most husbands' grasp. Many women are looking for "Prince Charming" to protect them and to slay the dragons in their lives. What woman wouldn't want an intelligent and sensitive husband who is confident in his life and work, and yet tender and loving at all the right times and places? As a husband, such expectations can be intimidating. How can any man meet them?

When men look around for encouragement from other men we see many of our peers struggling and failing in their marriages. Is it even possible to be the husband whom

God and our wives expect us to be?

God is no stranger to this inner anxiety, which becomes overwhelming at times. Through scripture, the Lord tells us: "Good news! You will not have to bear this yoke alone. I am with you always. And I have made a helper suitable for you!" God's design is for a wife to help and encourage her husband to be the best he can be for the Lord and for her. As he struggles toward maturity, each step of the way giving her the best he can offer, his wife is meant to walk with him, urging him on to still higher planes. God's intended result? Husbands give even more to their wives. This cycle of giving and receiving between husbands and wives is part of God's plan for marriage—a consistently uplifting experience!

Are you a giver? Are you first seeking the best from your mate before becoming a helper? Are your encouragement, and the positive contribution only you can give to your marriage, contingent upon first receiving something from your spouse? If so, take a few steps back and consider the wise, yet warmly practical advice which Dr. Juli Slattery provides in this long overdue love letter to wives who do not know how to help their husbands reach their potential.

Regrettably, America today is a hall of shame with breached trust, unfulfilled promises and vows, illusive intimacy, and broken lives in marriage. Countering this sad trend, Juli encourages wives to walk arm-in-arm with their husbands into a showcase of faithful, God-inspired marriages with mutual interaction and support. Thank God for her insights and encouragement!

Juli shows wives how they can proactively contribute their

thoughts, ideas and confidence without threatening their husbands' leadership. She explains how to find that delicate balance between being a strong and self-assertive woman, while also being able to trust and contribute to the strength of her husband with dignity, wisdom and courage. She reveals how many wives often misuse their much-needed influence by denying their power, which God gives them as a reservoir of strength for their mates. Alternatively, Juli warns of how wives sometimes can abuse their power by shattering their husbands' confidence, which inevitably leads to lonely and frustrating marriages.

I have known Juli and her wonderful husband, Michael, for a number of years now. While you may not have any way of knowing whether Juli practices what she preaches, I can assure you that she does. Her ideas and insights work!

Michelangelo once said that when he sees a block of stone, he sees a beautiful human figure struggling to come forth. With hammer and chisel in hand, he saw his mission as one who passionately set about the task of freeing the person within. Although we men may never admit it, too often we struggle with insecurities, doubt, anger or shame, which imprison us in a block of stone. With your loving service, and careful chipping and shaping of the block in which we are imprisoned, will you be the one to make a *Pieta* of your husband?

Don't let your well go dry. Don't be content to let your marriage be the death of your hopes and dreams. Instead, view it as a springboard—a launching pad to show the world what God can do through you, and for you and your mate.

Believe that you can, indeed, do everything through Christ who gives you strength. (Philippians 4:13) Be wise and build up your house in the spirit of Proverbs 31, as God honors and blesses your efforts. Fill yourself up from God's Word and the excellent advice to follow in this work of love from one who certainly is well qualified to counsel you on such matters.

—Joseph Warren Kniskern
attorney, family mediator,
author, *When the Vow Breaks: A Survival and Recovery Guide for Christians Facing Divorce* and *Courting Disaster: What Runaway Litigation Is Costing You, and What Can Be Done to Stop the Fallout*

Introduction

*T*here are more books devoted to marriage than practically any other subject imaginable. Is there anything to be discovered on the topic that has not already been exhausted? Communication, conflict, sex, in-laws, gender roles—countless experts have discussed them all. Ironically, amid the stacks of marriage books in Christian and secular bookstores, divorce continues to be a common event. Surprisingly, Christians are just as likely to divorce as the general population. In fact, truly happy marriages appear to be fewer and fewer. Surely there must be some remedy to help stop this epidemic.

Throughout history, wives have frequently been placed in the role of a victim. They have often felt helpless to change the relationships that hurt them the most. Authors, ministers and counselors typically emphasize the role of husbands in creating loving marriages. By default, wives are left waiting for their husbands to change their insensitive ways. There is no denying that a man has an awesome responsibility to provide and care for his wife. However, God has given a woman tremendous influence to shape her husband's development and attitude toward her. In fact, a wife's power may even be greater than her husband's within the marital relationship. This perspective is rarely emphasized, particularly within the church.

As recently as thirty years ago, many women believed that in order to be loving wives, they had to limit their own personal potential. Their intelligence and confidence were muted in order to allow their husbands to assume the role of protector and leader. Today, women have realized the freedom in thinking for themselves and using their gifts, talents and strengths.

When I was first married, I realized the difficult line I needed to walk in order to use my strength without threatening my husband's leadership. I struggled with the question, "How can I contribute my thoughts, ideas and confidence without taking over?" I noticed that many of my friends were asking similar questions.

My experience as a psychologist and speaker has confirmed to me that this is a pressing issue for contemporary Christian women. Time after time women have come to me for counseling, frustrated with the lack of intimacy in their marriages. The pattern I began to notice is that marital problems often revolved around this issue of a woman's strength. In some cases, she had buried her strength. Her "voice" was hardly audible under the dominant leadership of her husband. Other times, a woman had realized her strength, but used it in ways that were threatening to her husband.

I began tackling the issue of the power of godly women both personally and professionally. The response has been overwhelmingly positive. Although many of the women I counseled were hesitant to try my ideas at first, they agreed to use their strength in ways that supported and encouraged their husband's potential. They experimented with finding that delicate balance between being a strong woman and also one who is able to trust and contribute to the strength of another.

A wife's influence is an extremely powerful tool that can be used either to build her marriage or to destroy it. It has the potential to create both tremendous intimacy and raging resentment. As with any powerful weapon, its owner must understand how to use it appropriately. Unfortunately, very few women understand their power and how to direct it as God intended. Most wives are far from victims. Even in the midst of marital ruins, they have the resources to honor God, their husbands and themselves through dignity, wisdom and courage.

Because women are so unaware of their power to shape their marriages, they often misuse their influence. There are two vital mistakes a woman can make which can result in the destruction of her marriage. The first one is ignoring her power altogether. She denies that God has given her any substantial influence with her husband. In fact, she may even believe it is unbiblical to be a strong woman. This critical mistake results in a husband who has neither accountability, nor direction for the use of his leadership.

The second big mistake that a woman can make is to abuse her power. Even while a wife is convinced that she is a victim, she may be using her influence to destroy or discourage her husband. Whether through subtle or overt measures, it is easy for a woman to shatter her husband's confidence, trust in her and leadership ability through the misuse of her power in marriage.

Few husbands are willfully evil or destructive in their marriages. Their insensitivity and apathy typically result from their own insecurity, resentment or lack of understanding. Men desperately need their wives to use the influence they have to encourage and help them to become godly and loving husbands. Without it, both husband and wife are destined to a lonely and frustrating marriage.

As both a wife and a psychologist, I have learned that within every man is a hero. In some men that hero may be emerging; in others, he may be hidden deep beneath layers of shame, anger or doubt. Your job as a wife is to use your abilities and influence to promote the hero within your husband. It is neither an easy task, nor one that will be quickly accomplished. In fact, it may take a lifetime. However, there is no other way to achieve the intimacy and trust that you long for within your marriage.

You picked up this book for one of three reasons: to prepare for marriage, to strengthen a solid marriage or to prevent a failing marriage from dying. You may have a loving husband or you may be married to a tyrant. Although no book can be exhaustive on the subject of marriage, I pray that this book will encourage you regardless of your circumstances.

This work focuses exclusively on the role of a wife within marriage. Certainly, husbands contribute their share of misery to a marriage. But most wives can readily point out how their husbands need to change. A wife's greatest task is understanding how she should respond to the unique challenges within her marriage. Healing a relationship is not about finding fault, but on courageously embracing responsibility.

If you want to understand the power God has given you and how to use it in a way that honors Him and promotes intimacy, this book is for you. My prayer is that God has put this in your hands as a vehicle for awareness and practical changes in your marriage.

The wise woman builds her house, but with her own hands the foolish one tears hers down.

Proverbs 14:1, NIV

One

Do You Believe in Fairy Tales?

'm so tired of trying to make this marriage work! Year after year, we have had the same old arguments. Now, we rarely even talk about our problems. It's almost as if we have settled for a cold war. No passion. No excitement. Certainly no intimacy.

I always knew marriage wouldn't be perfect, but I expected it to be more fulfilling. John just doesn't seem to care anymore. He gets more excited about the latest football scores than he does about our relationship. He's more upset about losing a golf game than hurting my feelings. Even when he does something nice, I can tell he does it out of duty, not love. This isn't what marriage is supposed to be. I'm not sure I ever would have married had I known this is what I would get.

Sometimes I am so angry with John. We seem just a couple steps away from happiness, but we never get there. Why can't he realize how insensitive he is to my needs? Why can't he value the marriage as much as I do? Sometimes I don't even feel like it's worth trying any more. Did I make a mistake when I married him? Is there any hope for us?

—Kara, thirty-five
married for seven years

In my counseling practice, I hear far too many wives whose feelings could be expressed by this session with Kara. Hoping to find true love, they have found true frustration. Looking for happily ever after, they have endured enough disappointment to last a lifetime. Shattered dreams and unmet needs—what woman can't relate to them? With all that can be said of and for marriage, it rarely lives up to the dreams of many hopeful brides.

For instance, Emily had dreamed of marriage since she was a little girl. Her parent's marriage had lasted a mere four years after Emily was born. Even as an adult, she remembered the arguments and the yelling from her childhood. She could only imagine what it would be like to have a mom and dad who loved each other. Emily's hope for a loving family were soon invested in her dreams for intimacy and marriage. She wondered what kind of man she would marry and vowed that they would never be divorced.

After Emily grew up, her dreams were no less vivid. The drawers of her desk at work were stuffed with bride's magazines and romance novels—symbols of her longing for the perfect marriage. She hoped that everything bad about her life would disappear in the face of matrimony. The loneliness and pain would melt away when she was enveloped in the unconditional love of her "hero."

When Emily was twenty-five, her fantasy finally began to materialize. She met someone who appeared to be the man of her dreams. After a whirlwind courtship, the two were engaged with every hope of a match made in heaven. He seemed to complement her in every way, as his strengths compensated for her weaknesses. For awhile, her loneliness disappeared. Her fiancé seemed perfect, attentive to her thoughts and dreams.

The long-awaited day finally arrived. Walking down the aisle, Emily looked more beautiful than even she had imagined. Her prince was breathtaking in his tuxedo, his eyes filled with hope. In the secret recesses of her heart, she hoped that maybe she had discovered the impossible—true love. Their family and friends waved good-bye as the newlyweds fled to a romantic honeymoon getaway.

As the days and weeks of their new marriage wore on, the conflicts began to emerge. Emily's new husband was not nearly as attentive to her as he had been before they married. He spent hours in the garage, rebuilding an old car. Sometimes on Friday nights, he went out with the guys after work and came home after midnight. Emily felt the first shock of disappointment as the luster on her prince's armor began to tarnish. How could she be married, yet still have the same feelings of loneliness she had fought all of these years? Not wanting to make her husband angry, she swallowed her hurt and did every thing she knew to do to keep peace in the marriage.

By the time a year had passed, their marriage had become little more than a casual friendship. As Emily lay in bed one night, quietly sobbing into her pillow, she asked herself, "Did I marry the right person?" Every quality of her prince that had once reassured her now seemed to be collapsing into a heap of weaknesses. Panic seized her as she realized that her marriage was becoming just like that of her parents. Her fairy tale had evaporated.

Emily's story highlights the contrast between the romantic expectations of too many women and the reality of marriage. A naive young woman like Emily, determined not to make the same mistakes her parents had made but not knowing how to avoid them, would seem destined for disappointment. Her expectations for her husband were unrealistic. She did not anticipate conflict, anger and trials to be a part of her marriage. She was naturally crushed when the feelings of love began to waver.

But what about the older and more mature? Are they immune from unrealistic expectations and, therefore, more likely to be satisfied in marriage? Although they may be less surprised at the difficulty of marriage, older women are just as likely to be frustrated that their marriages are not more intimate.

Becky and Gene were in their mid-thirties when they got married. Because they wed later in life, they had fairly realistic expectations of what marriage would be. They had dated for over two years and had a good handle on their respective strengths and limitations. They knew that their big disagreements would always be over the issues of in-laws and money. Becky and Gene were prepared for marriage. They had every reason to be optimistic about their union and trusted God to bless their new family.

Becky came to me for counseling two years into the marriage. After only a few minutes, she collapsed into tears. "I am beginning to realize that Gene is never going to change. He will always be obsessed with work and he will never understand that I need more from him! I can't imagine living our whole lives together feeling this lonely. The worst part is that he doesn't even notice anything is wrong!"

Even if, like Becky, a woman thinks she is prepared for marriage, there will almost certainly come a point where she feels cheated. Something inside of her screams, "I deserve better than this!" Every thoughtless comment, forgotten birthday or sarcastic attitude reminds her of how broken her dream of fulfilling love seems to be. She wonders, "Is it my fault? Am I trying too hard or not hard enough? Why isn't this working the way it's supposed to?"

Marriage has been described as "a romance in which the hero dies in the first chapter." Many women, like Emily and Becky, are deeply wounded to learn that their dream of "the prince" exists only in fantasy. They may look enviously at other marriages and idolize husbands who are not their own, concluding that they simply picked the wrong man. They flock to seminars and workshops that promise three-step solutions to happiness, thinking, "If only I kiss my frog, he will turn into a prince." Like Cinderella in her dirty work clothes, they hope, "Somewhere is a fairy godmother who can make me beautiful enough to be cherished." The fantasy lives on—and so does the letdown.

The Biggest Obstacle to Intimacy

Overcoming the disappointment of marriage is a tremendous obstacle to building true intimacy. Often our understanding of love and marriage is unrealistic and incorrect. When we confront the real-life work of marriage, including disagreements, arguments and failures, we feel as if we have missed out on what we were promised.

Modern culture both influences our thinking and reflects our misconceptions about marriage. Think about much of the entertainment marketed for women, both young and old. Movies, television programs, cartoons and romance novels consistently tell a story of a woman searching for love. Finally, she finds Mr. Right. The stories almost always end when the man and women proclaim their love, with a wedding or at least a kiss to solidify their commitment. The message is clear: find the prince and you will become a princess. His love will rescue you. You will live happily ever after. No wonder girls and women alike often have an inaccurate view of both marriage and lasting love.

We recently took our two children to the magical land of Walt Disney World. At Cinderella's castle, we ate breakfast with many of the Disney characters. Cinderella and her handsome

Prince Charming fluttered through the room. When they got to our table, I playfully asked them about the state of their marriage. Prince Charming looked lovingly into his bride's eyes, held her hands, and said, "We have been married for fifty years and are still madly in love." I asked, "What is your secret?" "Living in Walt Disney World!" the Prince replied. Of course! Cinderella and Prince Charming are frozen in time. They have not aged or faced the realities of life. For fifty years, they have lived on their wedding day. In fact, they still wear the same clothes.

On the surface, their marriage seems perfect. The problem is that there is nothing more than the surface. Imagine that it were possible to live every day in the ecstasy of intoxicating new love. Never a fight or disagreement because there is never an issue to discuss. What a shallow existence! There has to be more to love than Cinderella's castle every day for fifty years.

Of course there is more to love. But it is never realized through escaping the reality of disappointment and conflict.

Newspaperman and novelist Edgar Watson Howe once said, "Marriage is a good deal like a circus: there is not as much in it as is represented in the advertising." Over time, most wives learn to live with their broken dreams and unfulfilled expectations. They accept that princes and princesses are fairy tales for children. "Adults live in the real world, with real relationships," they tell themselves. "Intimacy is simply unrealistic." Those who refuse to accept this reality may flit from marriage to marriage, hoping someday to win the lottery of love. Very few choose to believe that God can work wonders right in the middle of their all-too-human marriage. Why does God allow us to experience such disappointment? Why did He give us desires for love and intimacy that are destined to lead to disappointment?

Don't Give Up Hope

One of the greatest mysteries of human relationships is the miracle that God is able to work through a man and a woman who follow His design for marriage. The dream of the fairy tale stems from desires that God *can* fulfill. Our longings for love and intimacy highlight our need for relationships that go beyond the scope of the "normal" marriage. It is only through dependence on God and obedience to His plan (which is sometimes difficult) that we can get a glimpse of what real intimacy and love are all about. We are likely to find that mature love bears little resemblance to the tingles often mistaken as intimacy.

We long for intimacy, for the kind of love that believes and bears all things. We are starved for it. Although fairy tales and fantasies only serve to foster unrealistic hopes, the dream of intimacy is real and alive today. We live in homes, not castles, and there are no real dragons for our husbands to slay. But God has placed the yearning for intimacy in our hearts for a reason. He did not intend for us to be continually frustrated in our marriages. However, lasting intimacy does not develop based on the intoxication of new love.

God's plan is that a wedding displays love in its infancy, not its maturity. Intimacy can only grow and develop over a lifetime of living together within the safety of a committed love. Working through conflicts and differences, weathering storms, admitting selfishness and anger are all the necessary difficulties that allow genuine intimacy to grow. Unfortunately, many couples believe that such disappointments signal the end of intimacy instead of the beginning. *But the fairy tale must end for the potential of true intimacy to begin.*

I once heard a pastor say at a wedding ceremony, "There are hard marriages and there are bad marriages." Indeed, marriage takes hard work. It does not happen as naturally as falling in love. It is only through the longing for meaningful intimacy that people are reminded to work, to trust, to believe and to hope. A wife's desire for something deeper is often the engine that drives the couple to seek fulfillment. (However, if she allows her longing to turn into bitterness, she will contribute to the stifling loneliness she dreads.)

God has designed the mystery of intimacy to be achieved through two very imperfect humans. Couples exchanging their wedding vows are ordinary men and women who have normal weaknesses, vulnerabilities and insecurities—no matter how much they may wish to hide these inadequacies from each other. Both of them will soon learn the inevitability of disappointment. It is only through the acceptance of each other's faults that the love they dream of can begin to become a reality.

This is the central idea that I hope to share with you in this book: [*A woman never marries the man of her dreams. She helps the man she marries to become the man of his dreams.*]

One of my most enjoyable assignments as a counselor is working with engaged couples. Premarital counseling sometimes feels like what a doctor must experience when delivering a new baby. These young adults have not made any

When are we to love them for who they already are and when do we love them to change? We love them for who we know they can become in Christ??

mistakes yet. Their lives together are a clean slate filled with possibility and potential. The most exciting aspect of premarital counseling is the passion that they feel for each other. Their eyes see nothing but the strength and promise of their love.

Typically, I ask the future bride to discuss some concerns she has about her fiancé. More than once, a young woman has been unable to identify even one weakness of her future husband. Of course, her infatuation will not last. A day will soon come when this new bride will not have to think hard to pinpoint her husband's limitations.

Before the wedding, a woman sees a bright hope in her fiancé. She may see glimpses of his sensitivity, his strength and his commitment. After the wedding, she inevitably sees his weaknesses. Her disappointment may initially feel like a crashing blow. It becomes painfully obvious to her that he cannot meet all of her needs. She cannot believe how rude and insensitive he can be. Now she has a choice: to respond in anger to his weakness, or to invest with faith in his strength. For intimacy to grow, she must believe in his potential. (She can invest in the real-life prince that lies hidden beneath his doubts and insecurities.)

The secret of intimacy in marriage is not finding a hero *to be* your husband, but finding the hero *in* your husband. This is a tremendous and difficult task, particularly when a wife's reaction to her disappointment has been resentment. God has given each woman the power to help her husband grow, over time, into the godly man that he can become. Unfortunately, many women are so devastated by what he *is not* today that they refuse to invest in the man he *could become* tomorrow.

©2001 Julie Anderson.

What a Real Hero Looks Like

"Finding the *hero* in your husband." What does that mean? There is a lot of talk today about what makes a hero. How does one become a hero? Through special talents or athletic prowess? Superhuman feats? Daring rescues? If these are the criteria, where is the "hero" in the average husband?

The essence of heroics is the consistent choice to sacrifice for others. War heroes put their lives on the line for a military cause. Police officers and firefighters willingly place themselves in harm's way to protect others. Unsung heroes give up their own glory or desires in order to allow others to flourish. Jesus Christ is the ultimate hero. Not only did he give his life on the cross, but he spent his days on earth sacrificially ministering to the needs of others. This is exactly the role to which God has called every husband. He is to give himself to his wife, just as Christ gave Himself for the church. A husband's job is no easier than a wife's. He is called to be a daily hero.

Robertson McQuilkin's life represents the hero that every woman longs to discover in her husband. After forty years of marriage, his wife Muriel fell prey to Alzheimer's. At the time, Robertson was the president of Columbia International University. As Muriel's health faded, Robertson was forced with the choice of either putting her in an institution or retiring from his position to care for her full time. Here are his words about his decision:

As she needed more and more of me, I wrestled daily with the question of who gets me full-time—Muriel or Columbia Bible College and Seminary. . . . When the time came, the decision was firm. It took no great calculation. It was a matter of integrity. Had I not promised, forty-two years before, "in sickness and in health . . . till death do us part?" This was no grim duty to which I was stoically resigned, however. It was only fair. She had, after all, cared for me for almost four decades with marvelous devotion; now it was my turn. Such a partner she was! If

I took care of her for forty years, I would never be out of her debt. . . . She is such a delight to me. I don't have to care for her, I get to.

I have been startled by the response to the announcement of my resignation. Husbands and wives renew marriage vows, pastors tell the story to their congregations. It was a mystery to me until a distinguished oncologist, who lives constantly with dying people, told me, "Almost all women stand by their men; very few men stand by their women." Perhaps people sensed this contemporary tragedy and, somehow, were helped by a simple choice I considered to be my only option.

It is all more than keeping promises and being fair, however. As I watch her brave descent into oblivion, Muriel is the joy of my life. Daily, I discern new manifestations of the kind of person she is, the wife I always loved. I also see fresh manifestations of God's love—the God I long to love more fully.

(Christianity Today, *"Living by Vows"*)

Robertson McQuilkin is a hero. He did not save any lives, but he chose to use his as a reflection of God's love. He is an example of the heroic love wives long for in their husbands.

Finding the hero is not about depending on your husband for fulfillment. Ironically, it is only through letting go of the dream of his unfailing love that a woman can invest in the hope for true intimacy. It is not your husband that you must worship. The hero in your husband is only his capacity to image God's loving kindness, mercy and grace. To find that hero, you must know the God your husband was created to image. The fairy tale is not marrying Prince Charming. It is helping the man you married to become the godly man he is created to be.

As a wife, you have tremendous influence to either bring out the hero in your husband or bury it deeper within his anger and insecurity. God has given you the power to call forth your husband's valor or to highlight his faint-heartedness. Proverbs 14:1 (NIV) says, "The wise woman builds her house, but with her own hands the foolish one tears hers down." Are you using your influence to promote intimacy or to destroy any chance for it? The purpose of this book is to help you grasp the important role that you play in contributing to a fulfilling marriage. My prayer is that God will use these words to empower you in the challenging, lifelong tasks of building your home—of calling forth the hero in your husband.

Regardless of the state of your fairy tale, do not give up hope of fulfillment. God's plan for intimacy is real. It is available to those who seek the wisdom of His design for husband and wife. Nothing can guarantee a happy marriage. You cannot force your husband to love you, nor can you make your marriage an intimate one. You can only do your part. However, through your commitment to wisdom and faithfulness, you can participate in building your marriage rather than contributing to its destruction.

The wise woman builds her house, but with her own hands the foolish one tears hers down.

Proverbs 14:1, NIV

Questions for Discussion and Reflection

1. Try to remember back to your wedding day. What hopes and expectations did you have for your marriage? Which were realistic and which were not?

2. Which of your romantic dreams have come true? How have you been disappointed?

3. Why do you think God gave women the desire to be loved so completely only to be disappointed in marriage?

4. Read Proverbs 14:1. How might a wise woman build her house? How might a foolish woman tear hers down with her own hands? Why might she be so destructive to her own family?

5. Read Proverbs 1:24–32. What will happen to the woman who continues to ignore wisdom?

6. Read Proverbs 4:7–9, 9:10, 19:20, 2:6, and 8:34. How can a foolish woman become wise?

Two

Power for
a Purpose

*T*he strongest man in history was the Nazarene, Samson, whose life is recorded in the book of Judges. He was Mr. Israel, Mr. Solar System and Mr. Universe all wrapped up into one. Samson was a real-life superhero, able to kill a lion and defeat hundreds of men with his bare hands. Imagine being Samson's wife. How intimidating that would be! Believe it or not, Samson's wife was, in many ways, stronger than he was. In fact, it was the influence of two women that ultimately led to Samson's demise.

Samson married a Philistine woman whose name is not given in scripture. Although his parents advised him against uniting with this woman, Samson said to his father, "Get her for me. She is the right one for me" (Judges 14:3, NIV). At the beginning of the seven days of feasting at their wedding, Samson told a riddle to his Philistine guests. He made a wager with them that they would not be able to figure out the riddle within the seven days. The Philistines ordered Samson's new wife to find out the answer to the riddle. She begged, cried and manipulated Samson into revealing the solution to her. She immediately told the Philistines the answer and they won the bet. The wedding festival was never completed, because Samson's fiancée became the wife of his best man.

Samson was filled with anger, and God gave him the strength to single-handedly kill 1,000 Philistines. Samson learned a great lesson about his weakness with women. Or did he? Twenty years later, Samson fell in love again with another beautiful Philistine woman named Delilah. The Philistines bribed Delilah to find out the secret of Samson's strength. Samson toyed with her, making up three lies about how he could become as weak as a normal man. Delilah, being the faithful companion that she was, gave away his secret each of the three times. Samson had to know that she would readily betray him again, but Delilah put her feminine powers into full gear. She manipulated him by saying, "How can you say, 'I love you,' when you won't confide in me? This is the third time you have made a fool of me and haven't told me the secret of your strength" (Judges 16:15, NIV). It is a wonder that Samson never questioned her love after she had betrayed his confidence three times!

When Samson's will proved strong, Delilah turned to nagging. "With such nagging, she prodded him day after day until he was tired to death" (Judges 16:16, NIV). Finally, he relented and told Delilah the truth. The secret to his strength was that, in obedience to God's command, his hair had never been cut. Of course, Delilah stayed true to her character and told his secret. His enemies swiftly conquered Samson. They poked his eyes out, and ridiculed him and his God.

What an amazing story! I can see the headlines of *The Philistine Gazette:* "Mr. Universe becomes a wimp at the hands of his mistress." Samson's wife and Delilah were both stronger than he was because they capitalized on his vulnerability. They used their influence to tempt Samson into forsaking his vows and commitment to God. In essence, they held the power to bring down an entire nation through their influence.

As profound as this story is, it has happened repeatedly all over the world since the beginning of time. Women have wielded incredible influence over big, strong, powerful men. Although generals, governors and presidents have been traditionally males, the women in their lives have had much to do with how these men have led. Only occasionally is this influence overtly recognized. The wives of America's presidents are a good example of this. Although all First Ladies have had a pronounced influence on their husband's leadership, most have not caught the attention of the public. However, a few have been open about their influence. Nancy Reagan was a very influential person in her husband's life. In fact, she was quite involved in his administration behind the scenes. The most recent example of this is the powerful Hillary Clinton. Clearly, she played a large role in her husband's political successes and moral failures. The press openly referred to Bill and Hillary as the "First Couple" or co-presidents, joking about getting "two for the price of one."

Speaking of First Couples, Satan clearly understood the influence of a wife. He never spoke directly to Adam, but approached Eve instead. Once he had convinced Eve to partake of the forbidden fruit, she easily persuaded Adam to join her in sin. Ever since the Garden of Eden, wives have been influencing their husbands daily for both good and evil. Ralph Waldo Emerson once said, "A man's wife has more power over him than the State."

A Wife's Influence Originates from Her Husband's Needs and Desires

Most women are quite aware of their own needs within marriage. However, they may be hard pressed to articulate what their husbands actually need and desire from them. The truth is, men are as needy as women are. They depend on their wives for both physical and emotional necessities. A man's need naturally translates into a woman's power. The greater the need, the greater the power.

The electric company has a lot of power over us. (No pun intended!) We need electricity and there is only one source to supply it. Therefore, we are largely at the mercy of our local electric company. They have the power to charge whatever they deem fair. If we do not pay our electric bill, they shut off our electricity. This is why the electric bill is usually the first to be paid. They get what they want (our money) because they have what we need (electricity).

This principle also applies to relationships. When one person becomes dependent upon another person for emotional survival, he or she is at the mercy of the one who can meet those needs. Husbands and wives, by God's design, trust each other for many of their needs to be met. In some marriages, a wife is dependent upon her husband for most of her physical needs because he earns the majority of the money. Although not as obvious as a paycheck, the needs of husbands for their wives is every bit as significant. These needs open the door for influence of a wife over her husband. There are three primary areas in which a husband's needs will result in a healthy dependence on his wife.

She Completes Him

In the Garden of Eden, God saw that Adam, by himself, was not "complete." After creating Adam, God said, "It is not good for the man to be alone; I will make him a helper suitable for him" (Genesis 2:18, NIV). God created Eve to be a helper for Adam. Her assistance to him was not simply to keep him company as he strolled around the garden. It also included helping him accomplish the work that God had given him. The word "helper" can also be translated as "completer." There are subtle differences in the ways that God designed a man and a woman. These differences were intended to complement and complete each other. She is the perfect counterpart for him, providing for what he lacks.

(Although husbands are placed in the position of leadership in the home, they are not to lead alone.) A husband needs the input and perspective of his wife when making decisions. The basic differences in men and women suggest that for him to make decisions without her input would be like operating with half a brain, (And vice versa)

What would your wedding have been like if your husband planned it? What would your house look like if he decorated it? What would your family eat if he were in charge of meal planning? How would he celebrate birthdays, plan the social calendar and keep in touch with extended family if it were only he? My guess is that the picture formed in your mind in answer to most of these questions is quite humorous. Men and women simply approach life differently. The things that matter to her are typically different than what occupies his mind. A man's life is usually drastically changed by the feminine influence of his wife.

Andy is a man many would characterize as the "typical male," focused on goals and driven to achieve them. Although Andy was a natural success at business, he ran into difficulty expressing his feelings and showing sensitivity toward others. Andy fell in love with Beth and the two married. In many ways, Beth and Andy could not be more different. She was extremely sensitive and invested in people, while Andy was the proverbial bull in the china shop. Through Beth, a new world emerged for Andy. She taught him about her feelings and how he could meet her needs. Beth also helped Andy understand his feelings and how his behavior affected others. She asked him questions about why success was important to him and why he lost his temper during arguments. When children came, Beth's example and encouragement helped Andy become a loving and sensitive father. Andy came to rely on Beth's influence. She opened up another dimension of living for Andy that helped him become a more "complete" person.

Unique individual differences also play a key role in teamwork. In some cases, a wife may be better at long-range planning, while the husband relies upon spontaneity. A wife may be more social, more talkative or more serious than her husband. Two perspectives and two sets of unique strengths are definitely better than one. A team approach will help the couple to successfully navigate through the thousands of decisions involved in the daily life of budgeting, managing a house, child rearing and relating.

An aspect of completing also includes accountability. Ecclesiastes 4:9–10 says: "Two are better than one because they have a good return for their labor. For if either of them falls, the one will lift up his companion. But woe to the one who falls when there is not another to lift him up." (NIV)

I can think of several times in our marriage when both Mike and I have needed each other to lift up one another. Whether it is a spiritual struggle, a moral temptation or just a difficult time, having the other person there has been crucial. Sometimes it was a word of encouragement, a timely warning or even a kick in the pants. Woe to the man (or woman) who does not have another to lift him up when he falls.

The need for a "completer" in marriage naturally gives a wife influence. Without his wife's help and perspective, a man will be less effective at work, with his children, in his relationships and in knowing himself. A wife's influence and input can be extremely powerful. She teaches him about aspects of life and relationships that would otherwise be lost to him. A wise woman uses her position of influence carefully and prayerfully. Bad advice or misguided input, even if it is well intended, can be as harmful as good advice is helpful.

She Admires Him

Endless hours of watching baseball, basketball, football and hockey have inspired boys of all ages to fantasize about what it would be like to be that star athlete basking in the limelight. We've all watched little boys in their backyards acting out their dream of throwing the touchdown pass that wins the Super Bowl, or hitting the home run that wins the World Series. In their eyes, this feat is similar to saving the world from destruction.

Just as men dream of being the hero, they also fear becoming the "goat" who lets the whole world down. What about the quarterback who threw an interception or the slugger who struck out to end the big game? For every athlete who wins, one loses. To play the game means taking that risk. By becoming a husband, each man plays the game hoping to be a hero, but secretly he fears he is really a goat. Although he brings into the game his own talents and shortcomings, success as the leader of his family depends largely on what he needs from his wife: her confidence.

Although some men have been raised to project a facade of strength, every man carries within him a fragile sense of worth and competence. He constantly walks a tightrope, striving to prove that he is adequate and capable. Although failures in

business and friendship may wound him, (nothing is more devastating than to be viewed as incompetent by the woman of his
life.) Conversely, the most exhilarating and empowering gift a
wife can give is to trust and believe in her husband. How?

Even in the face of public success, a husband can feel like
a failure if his wife cannot or will not trust him. The opposite
is also true. In the middle of a temporary failure, a husband
can feel like a hero if his wife skillfully and consistently
believes in him.

In his classic work, *Seasons of a Man's Life,* Daniel
Levinson talks about a young man and his "dream." According
to Levinson, every man has a dream. His dream may be as
specific as a business objective he would like to reach, but it
also includes intangibles representing what the man would
someday like to become. The young man's dream is a central
part of who he is. It deeply affects his relationships. One of his
greatest needs is to find a woman who supports and embraces
his dream. She believes he can become his dream, and she
commits herself to helping him actualize it. She walks with
him every step of the way, giving him the encouragement and
feedback that he will need to remain committed to his dream.

Your husband needs you to support him as he takes the risks
necessary to work toward his dream. When he experiences
success, he wants to look over and see you smiling, sharing his
joy. When he is tired and discouraged, struggling against the
odds, he wants to know there is still one person believing in
him and willing him to keep trying.

Like anything else, becoming a husband, a provider and a
leader is a process. Your husband will fail along the way. Your

respect means that you continue to believe and invest in his strength—even when everyone else gives up on him.

Although a husband may appear to be independent and self-sustaining, he desperately needs the admiration and approval of his wife. He longs to be the most wonderful man in the world to her. His work is greatly diminished if she does not support it. He becomes disenchanted and withdrawn if his wife does not praise him as a loving husband and father.

William Butler Yeats said, "I have spread my dreams under your feet; tread softly because you tread on my dreams." A wife certainly has her husband's dreams beneath her feet, to nourish or to stomp upon. She has great power to grant or withhold approval from him.

Some friends once told me a story about a man they met while traveling. Tom, an elderly man who was staying in the same hotel, immediately came to the attention of everyone around him. He was loud, obnoxious and rude. My friends watched from afar as Tom yelled at waitresses and ordered that his food be taken back. They bravely decided to approach and befriend Tom to discover what made him so angry. They began to smile at him while passing and make friendly comments. After a few days of this, they invited Tom to eat lunch with them and he accepted.

My friends showed a genuine interest in Tom and asked questions about his life. They discovered that he was a wealthy man who lived in St. Louis and was vacationing in Miami at the advice of his physician due to his failing health. Tom's children were alienated from him and his marriage was a wreck. Although Tom and his wife were not fond of each other, he had pleaded with her to come with him to Miami. He described feeling utterly rejected by her when she refused to join him, as she had many times before. Throughout their marriage, Tom's wife had consistently rejected and ridiculed him, leaving him a lonely, bitter man.

On the surface, Tom had everything a man could desire. He had achieved great power, status and wealth. Yet he was miserable. Although other factors had certainly contributed to Tom's frail emotional state, his broken marriage was at the center of his heartache.

The kindness and respect that my friends showed Tom deeply affected him. He was so hungry for approval and love that he frequently sought them out during his stay in Miami. He even offered to exchange his suite for their standard room. Though they gratefully refused, they learned when they went to check out of the hotel a few days later that Tom had paid their entire bill.

Obviously, my friends only heard Tom's side of this story. He certainly shared the responsibility for the failure of his marriage. Over the years, his obsession with work and his inconsiderate manner must have deeply wounded his wife. Had my friends met Tom's wife, they may have felt equally empathetic for her unhappiness. Regardless of how or why their marriage disintegrated, Tom was destroyed by his wife's rejection of him. In the middle of all of his worldly "success" he felt like a failure.

No matter how successful or confident a man may seem, he still desperately needs the admiration and approval of his wife. Nothing can replace this! This gives a wife great power to grant or withhold approval. Therefore, she must be very careful about how she uses it. A woman can choose to use this power either to build her husband up or to tear him down. It is tempting for a woman to withhold approval from her husband for her own selfish reasons. For example, she may withhold her approval of her husband's work because he does not make enough money to live in a nice neighborhood. Perhaps she subtly withholds her admiration because she is angry about something he said last week. This misuse of power can be devastating to the trust that must be present in a marriage in order for intimacy to occur.

She Arouses Him

Several years ago, my husband and I attended a flourishing church. The pastor of the church was clearly a dynamic person who appeared to have a sincere heart for the Lord. One day, I opened the newspaper to discover that our pastor had been arrested for soliciting prostitution. I was astonished and deeply disappointed. This man had everything to lose by his actions—a loving wife, several wonderful children and a vibrant ministry. His life of spiritual leadership and his family were ravaged by his actions.

Unfortunately, this story is not an isolated incident. There are countless stories of Christian men who betray all that they hold dear to satisfy sexual desires. To women, this behavior often defies understanding. They fail to comprehend the alluring influence of the sexual drive in the lives of their husbands.

The book of Proverbs is filled with admonitions to men to

avoid sexual temptations. Perhaps no subject is mentioned more often by Solomon. Scripture provides many examples of great men who succumbed to inappropriate sexual activity, including Samson, David and even Solomon himself. The image of the female body has a magnetic power over a man. The sight of a beautiful, sensual woman can influence his thinking and behavior. (In addition, men have a physiological need for sexual outlets, more so than women do) A woman who is able to tap into that need, awakening her husband's sexual desires, potentially has enormous influence.

Some women have made an art of enhancing the power of their sexuality. They overtly exude sensuality through their build, attire, speech and movements. Cleopatra is regarded as one of the most influential women in history. Her power largely resulted from her ability to seduce the male leaders of her time.

The word "seduction" often carries a negative connotation in the minds of many women. Seduction is something that a wife may think happens exclusively outside of her marriage. Her husband's sexuality may be a primary concern, as she fears that he is vulnerable to being seduced by another woman. It does not have to be this way. Although a man's sexuality may create anxiety for his wife, it is potentially an area of great influence for her. While a woman may never think of seducing her husband, only she is able to arouse and satisfy all of his sexual needs within the context of a committed relationship. In fact, he depends upon her to sexually fulfill him. This is tremendous power.

Some women forfeit this area of influence in their marriage. Surrounded by pressures at home, with children and at work, a wife may have little time and energy to invest in her sensuality or physical appearance. As the marriage wears on, as stress builds, as age (and gravity!) takes its natural effect, a wife may give up any hope of being sexual. This is particularly true if there are problems in the marriage. Why should she invest in meeting his needs for arousal or sexual fulfillment when he never even takes the time to meet her emotional needs?

Although this reaction is common and, in many cases, understandable, it is unwise. A wife who gives up sexually must realize that, by doing so, she is giving her influence to other sexual outlets such as fantasy, pornography, and possibly, other women. Since she will not meet his needs for arousal and fulfillment, sexual temptations have greater power over her husband. Instead, a wife can enhance her influence with her husband by embracing it. She can take the initiative with actions such as wearing clothes that he likes, maintaining attractiveness or responding when he initiates. This may sound unrealistic to some. However, by owning her sexual power, a woman reduces the influence of outside sexual temptations, makes herself more precious to her husband and feels more sensual and feminine herself. (Chapter 11 addresses this topic more completely.)

Certainly, there is much more to a sexual relationship than power. God never intended sex to be used as a weapon or form of manipulation. Both husbands and wives can experience tremendous fulfillment through their sexual relationship. However, women must be aware of the influence that their sexuality contributes in marriage.

As with any other area of influence, a wife can misuse this power. She can use her ability to arouse her husband for her own benefit. For example, she may subtly arouse him, then withhold sex because he disagreed with her earlier in the day. Some women refuse sexual activity when they are not completely satisfied in their marriage. Although it is good for a wife to maximize her sexual influence with her husband, she must be careful to use it to enhance intimacy in their relationship rather than to destroy it.

But I Don't Feel Powerful!

Sarah came to counseling a defeated woman. She avoided eye contact and her voice was barely audible while she told her story. The mother of three children, she had been married to Keith for twelve years. Their marriage had steadily disintegrated over time. According to Sarah, Keith was a dominating, controlling man. He was loud and demanding of Sarah and the children. When he yelled at her, Sarah felt like a little child, helpless to protect herself. She experienced no degree of influence or power as a wife.

Many women, like Sarah, marvel at the thought that God has given them influence as wives. In their minds, they think they are the exception. They feel absolutely powerless in their marriages. For a variety of reasons, some women fear their power and bury it in their intimate relationships. Other women marry men who are afraid of being challenged or questioned by their wives. Over time, these women learn that to keep the peace, they must mute their influence. With each day, they surrender more of their strength until the marriage begins to resemble a dictatorship or a parent-child relationship.

Still other women have great influence with their husbands, but are unaware of their power. Sharon was a depressed woman in her early forties. She and her husband, David, had five children. Sharon was convinced that she was powerless over all situations in her family. She felt trapped in what she perceived as her role of perpetual servant to her family. From the time she woke up until the time she went to bed, she sacrificed her needs to meet those of her husband and children. Sharon was miserable—and everyone around her knew it! On the surface, she appeared to be the giving, submissive wife. In reality, she was seething with anger. She felt controlled by David, who depended on her for his every need.

Through counseling, Sharon learned that she had tremendous difficulty saying "no" when asked to take care of something. Over time, she had defined herself as a martyr who dutifully put all of her needs aside for the sake of others. She had perfected the art of making David feel guilty for her service to him. Although on the surface Sharon seemed powerless, she, in fact, had used her influence to create the very situation she despised. Sharon needed to be needed and pitied for her great sacrifices. Although her martyr role resulted in depression and alienation, she was unwilling to relinquish it.

A woman's feeling of powerlessness may be very real. However, it does not nullify the fact that she is extremely influential in her marriage. The very fact that a wife does not use her influence has a powerful impact on her marriage, and on her husband's development as a man. *Every wife will make a difference in her husband's life, even through her refusal to use her influence.* This means that every wife must choose whether she will use her influence to build her house or to tear it down.

God's Design for a Wife's Power

Power has become an ugly word to many Christians. This is especially true of Christian women. Picture in your mind what a powerful woman might look like. She may be big and strong. Perhaps she is seductive, or maybe conniving. Power seems to describe the opposite of the feminine, submissive wife that some Christian women want to become. The concept of a woman's power within marriage is something that is rarely discussed because it is confusing and in many cases scary. But let's be honest. Women use their power every day, one way or another. Let's call it what it is instead of pretending that it does not exist.

The influence that a woman has in her marriage is not only real, but it is by design. As discussed earlier in this chapter, Genesis 3 shows Eve influencing Adam to eat the fruit. Even before the fall, Eve had tremendous influence with her husband. Adam still made his own decision, but Eve had a profound impact on his choice. In the perfect world of Eden, God gave Eve power in her relationship with her husband. This influence is by God's design.

Wives often influence their husbands in destructive ways. However, there are some beautiful illustrations in scripture of godly women using their God-given influence to help their husbands grow in wisdom and godliness. Queen Esther is one of them.

Esther was married to King Ahasuerus. Before he married Esther, King Ahasuerus was married to a woman named Vashti. On one occasion, King Ahasuerus held a big party for many of the powerful men around him. He wanted to display his beautiful wife, Vashti, for the guests at his party, but she refused. As a result, King Ahasuerus was humiliated in front of his guests and, eventually, had Vashti banished for her behavior. In time, King Ahasuerus selected Esther to be Vashti's replacement because of Esther's beauty.

After she was married to King Ahasuerus, Esther discovered that an evil man named Hamaan had persuaded King Ahasuerus to kill all of the Jews because they did not obey the laws of the king. At the time, King Ahasuerus did not know that his wife, Esther, was a Jew.

Esther was understandably horrified when she heard of her husband's decision. She believed that God had put her in the position of great influence to save her people from death, and she asked all of the Jews to pray for her.

Esther was in a precarious situation. She could not approach the king unless he asked for her. If she initiated a meeting, the king had the power to have Esther killed. However, she believed that she must use her influence to change the terrible decision that her husband was about to make.

Summoning her courage, Esther decided to invite King Ahasuerus to a banquet in his honor. She dressed in royal robes and displayed tremendous respect as she entered the king's presence, and her invitation was met with favor. In fact,

King Ahasuerus was so pleased with Esther's banquet that he told her he would give her anything she asked for. Knowing her husband, she responded by inviting him to yet another banquet. At the second banquet, King Ahasuerus again asked Esther what he could give her. At this point, Esther revealed Hamaan's plan and pleaded with the king to save the Jews. King Ahasuerus immediately protected Esther's people and sentenced Hamaan to death.

The influence of his godly wife saved King Ahasuerus from making a terrible decision. On his own, he was unable to assess that Hamaan was an evil man and a poor advisor. He also was not sensitive to the plight of the Jewish people. Esther prayerfully used her God-given power as the king's wife to influence him in a way that no other person could. She *completed* him by giving him a perspective that he would have otherwise missed.

Esther also *admired* her husband. Unlike Vashti, Esther showed the king great respect in the way that she approached him in front of others. She did not abuse her position as his wife. As a result, King Ahasuerus wanted to please her. Esther essentially told her husband that he could please her by making a merciful decision.

Finally, Esther *aroused* her husband. King Ahasuerus had chosen her because of her beauty. Her physical appearance allowed her to be in a unique position to influence her husband. Whereas Vashti used her beauty to humiliate and reject the king, Esther used hers to please, honor and influence him.

There are many differences between the modern wife and Queen Esther. Fortunately, wives today can initiate a conversation with their husbands without being afraid of death. Also, their husbands are not usually making decisions about whether or not to annihilate thousands of people! Though less dramatic, a modern wife's influence has a major impact on her husband's practical, moral and spiritual decisions every single day. God has given a wife this power for the purpose of *building* her house! She is to use her strength, beauty, intelligence and intuition to *empower* her husband. Like Esther, she can carefully use her influence in all three areas to help her husband grow in character and godliness.

The World's Distortion of a Wife's Power

Unfortunately, examples of godly women using their influence to support and empower their husbands are rare. Christian women are afraid of words like power and influence for good reasons. Everywhere they look, women can see glaring examples of marriages destroyed by the misuse of power. A strong woman is often understood as a wife who controls and dominates her husband.

Everything in our world that God created has the potential to be distorted. Music can glorify God or profane Him. Money can build a church or destroy the character of a nation. The law can protect the innocent or restrict freedom. A woman's influence is no exception to this rule. What God intended for good has been used by some to destroy His design for marriage and oneness.

The first way that a woman can destroy her house is by using her power to sabotage her husband's role as the leader in the family. It is absolutely impossible for a wife to show her husband the respect he needs if she challenges him for leadership. It communicates that he is incompetent and that she does not trust him.

A wife also can bring destruction to her home by refusing to use her influence as a wife. A husband needs his wife to *complete* him as his companion, to *admire* and encourage his leadership and to *arouse* and fulfill him sexually. If she gives up her influence in any of these three areas, her husband becomes increasingly vulnerable to making unwise decisions and developing destructive patterns in their family.

Ignore it, avoid it or call it something different—but a wife cannot escape the fact that she has great influence in her relationship with her husband. The power that she possesses is God-given. She can use it to empower him toward godliness and intimacy, she can abuse it or she can bury it. The choice is hers—to build her house or tear it down with her own hands.

The wise woman builds her house, but with her own hands the foolish one tears hers down.

Proverbs 14:1, NIV

Questions for Discussion and Reflection

1. Why is it so difficult for Christian women to embrace their power within marriage? What stereotypes does a powerful woman challenge?

2. Do you have any reservations about being a "powerful" woman in your marriage? If so, what are they?

3. Read the story of Esther. How did Queen Esther use her power to *complete, admire* and *arouse* her husband? How might she have used her power to harm him instead of helping him?

4. In what way do you have power to complete your husband? What do you offer to him through your personality, talents, perspective and femininity? How might you be using this influence to harm rather than help him? What are some concrete ways in which you can help him by completing him?

5. In what areas does your husband need you to admire him? Think of times that you have been tempted to withhold approval from him. How can you actively use your power to meet his need to feel competent as a provider? Husband? Friend? Father?

6. In what ways does your sexuality give you power in your marriage? Do you believe this is by God's design? How can you use this power in ways that honor God?

Three

Submission:
A Four-Letter Word?

I, Julianna, take you, Michael, as my lawful wedded husband. I promise to love, honor and submit . . ." Wait a minute! How did that word *submit* get into my wedding vows? No one ever told me I would have to submit!

Many couples are rewriting their vows to avoid traditional words like "till death us do part." However, no word is more unpopular in a wedding than *submission*. Several women friends who attended my wedding were flabbergasted that I had uttered such a dreadful promise. "I can't believe you said that," they exclaimed several weeks later. "Did you actually mean that you would submit to him? You can't be serious!"

Perhaps no word in the English language has created

more confusion and frustration for women than *submission*. It has been a driving force behind the feminist movement—and for good reason. The concept of a wife's submission in marriage has been bent and twisted in so many ways that most people do not have an inkling of what it really means.

Tina's husband, Jim, has a bad temper. He sometimes yells at the children when he is frustrated at work, or while he's wrestling with a household project. The kids are obviously hurt by his anger and insensitivity. Should Tina intervene? How can she do this in the spirit of submission?

Sam has never been happy at work. Over the course of ten years, he has had nine different jobs and moved his family seven times. Should his wife Laura continue to follow him every time he becomes discontent at work? If she does, is she being submissive or foolish? Should she even tell Sam her objections and concerns? Should she give him an ultimatum?

Jerry, Ashley's husband, uses very little discretion when it comes to what his children watch on television. He often brings home R-rated movies and views them in front of their young children. Although Ashley is bothered by Jerry's insensitivity, she does not know how to put her foot down. At church, she has heard about the importance of having a submissive and quiet spirit. What should she do?

The list of examples is endless. Although submission sounds like an abstract and lofty word, it is, in fact, a very practical aspect of marriage. Every wife makes daily decisions about how she supports her husband's leadership, based on her understanding and acceptance of God's command to her. Misunderstanding the meaning of submission and when it should be applied can lead to devastation in a marriage. When a wife, in the spirit of submission, buries her influence and power, she may enable her husband to become a controlling and dominating tyrant. If a wife fails to submit when she should, she will reverse God's order for marriage, causing her husband to feel both inferior and angry. Perhaps nothing determines the level of intimacy that develops between a couple more profoundly than the balanced and true application of this tricky concept.

What Submission Is Not

Probably the most effective way of addressing what submission really *is*, is to discuss briefly what it *is not*. In fact, most women cringe at the thought of submission largely because they misunderstand what it really means. Frankly, if submission meant what many people believe it to mean, I would want no part of it!

Submission Does Not Mean That Women Are Less Valuable Than Men

Every woman reading these words has been affected in some way by the feminist movement. Its influence is inescapable. When they began, feminists were reacting to a society that misunderstood and abused the biblical command that women submit to their husbands. Over the past couple of centuries, submission has been interpreted to suggest that women are less valuable, less intelligent and less significant as human beings than men are. In the past and until more recently in some cultures, even the law viewed wives as the property of their husbands. They were given no more rights than children or farm animals.

Of course, some women have thrown out the baby with the bath water. Instead of seeking an appropriate understanding of women's roles within marriage, many have rejected the concept of submission altogether. Although they overlooked the inherent differences between men and women, feminists were right to fight for a high regard of women. God views women as no less valuable or capable than men. In fact, He has created women with unique abilities that are meant to compensate for male inadequacies.

The Bible states clearly that both men and women were created in the image of God. Although men and women are different in many respects, they are the same in their status as a special creation. Both were set apart as distinct from all of God's other masterpieces. Men and women uniquely express aspects of God's character through their ability to choose, their eternal souls and their creative abilities.

Christ's ministry while on earth clearly demonstrated the value that He placed on women. Many of His encounters recorded in the Gospel were with women. If they were less valuable than men, why did Jesus spend so much time ministering to their souls and addressing their concerns? He treated women with even greater dignity than His culture demanded.

God placed women in the submissive role in marriage for a purpose. The reason He did this is not because women are less valuable. In fact, scripture instructs husbands to treat their wives with great respect for their value and dignity. Husbands are called to lay down their lives for their wives, even as Christ laid down His life for the church.

Submission Does Not Mean That Women Should Not Share Their Opinions

I was driving in the car recently, listening to a Christian radio station, when I heard something that astounded me. A lady who was teaching on submission said emphatically that a woman should never give her opinion on anything unless her husband asks for it. I can certainly understand the spirit of this teaching. Men usually do react badly when their wives are constantly telling them what to do and second-guessing their decisions. However, there are many situations in which a woman should give her opinion, even if it is unsolicited.

Laura and Bob were trying to decide whether or not to build an addition onto their house. They had three children who were sharing one room, and the house only had one bathroom. Such a large decision certainly required a lot of thought and planning. Could they afford the addition? Would it be cheaper just to move? If they did build it, who should design it?

What do you think would happen if Bob made all of these decisions without ever getting any of Laura's input? Maybe Bob is the type to do things impulsively, or maybe he just does not naturally think of including Laura. If he leaves her out, for whatever reason, Laura's lack of input is likely to be harmful on many levels. Most importantly, she will become quite angry and resentful that her opinion did not even count. After all, she has to live in that house on their budget just as much as Bob does.

Bob ultimately may disagree with Laura's opinion. Laura could probably live with the decision, even if Bob decides to do something different than what she thought they should. However, their relationship will be severely threatened if she does not feel like an important member of the team.

More than having things always go their way, most women just want to be heard. They want to be understood and to have their thoughts and feelings validated. In fact, it is impossible for a husband to show his wife love if she does not regularly teach him what she needs through expressing her feelings and opinions.

There is one woman in scripture who is pointed out by the apostle Peter as an example of a submissive wife: Abraham's wife, Sarah (I Peter 3:6). Although Sarah clearly followed

Abraham's leadership, scripture records two specific times when she gave her unsolicited opinion. Sarah was getting older and was convinced that she could not give Abraham the child that God had promised to him. She told Abraham to sleep with her maid, Hagar, in order to have a child. Genesis 16:2 says, "Abraham agreed to what Sarah said."

Hagar became pregnant, giving Abraham a son. They both realized that this had been a bad decision. It caused great tension in the family between Sarah and Hagar. Eventually, Sarah became pregnant and had Isaac, who was the fulfillment of God's promise. Sarah and Isaac continued to struggle with Hagar and her son, Ishmael. Sarah told Abraham of the tension within the house and said, "Get rid of that slave woman and her son, for that slave woman's son will never share in the inheritance with my son Isaac." Abraham at this point was not sure what to do. God then said to Abraham, "Do not be so distressed about the boy and your maidservant. Listen to whatever Sarah tells you, because it is through Isaac that your offspring will be reckoned" (Genesis 21:10–12, NIV).

Sarah, our example of a submissive woman, clearly played an active role in her home. She respected Abraham and gave him the final authority to make decisions, but she did not withhold her feelings and opinions. In at least one instance, God encouraged Abraham to listen to her.

Submission Does Not Mean Blind Obedience

The words submission and obedience are often used interchangeably. In fact, less than a century ago, wedding vows often used the word "obey" rather than "submit." The Greek words for obey and submit are different and communicate subtly different messages.

The word translated as "obey" is used to describe the relationship between children and their parents. To obey means to listen and act without questioning the recognized authority. In contrast, submission is a willing act of placing oneself under the authority of another. Christ is our perfect example of submission. He willingly submitted His desire to His Father's authority by coming to earth, suffering and dying on the cross.

When children obey, they naturally assume that the guidance of their parents is right and appropriate. They are not to question what their parents tell them to do. Obviously, this changes as children become adults. Instead of obeying, they are commanded to honor their parents.

Parents have authority over their young children because they have wisdom and understanding that their children lack. My three-year-old son has no concept of why he needs to eat vegetables. Of course, we tell him that they help him to grow stronger and to be healthy. His little mind has a very limited understanding of physical strength and health. What if one day he decides that we don't know what we're talking about? From now on, he will only eat candy and Doritos because they taste good. In his reasoning, this makes sense. However, at this point of his life, his reasoning does not count. There is no room for him to question our authority. We must make decisions that he is incapable of making. He is in our parental care. As parents, God entrusts us to make good decisions for him.

A wife, on the other hand, is a different story. She has the same ability to reason and make moral and responsible decisions as her husband. She can, in fact, think for herself. The command to submit to her husband does not mean that she turns off her brain. She willingly and thoughtfully commits to giving him a place of leadership. However, she can and should reason with him if he is making decisions that seem to contradict what she understands as moral, correct and wise.

The law reflects this important distinction. Imagine that a father asks a small child to go into a bank, point a gun at the teller and demand money. Who will go to jail? The father is responsible for the child's behavior. He likely will be severely punished, while the child will be treated with greater leniency by the law. Now imagine that a husband asks his wife to rob the bank. If she is caught, can she plead innocence because her husband told her to rob the bank? Of course not. She will be judged in a manner that reflects her own ability to make good decisions, regardless of what her husband told her to do.

Submission Does Not Mean a Dictatorship

Unfortunately, many women believe that they are being submissive by playing a weak and passive role with their husbands. They let their husbands make all of the decisions and allow them to control every aspect of the family. This posture does nothing to promote intimacy in marriage. In fact, it invariably leads to the unbalanced relationship of a "dictator" and a "doormat." When a wife denies her influence in the marriage, she grants her husband total control of the family. Although she may believe she is doing him a favor, she is actually setting him up for failure. He cannot effectively lead without her input, encouragement, support and accountability. The more inadequate he feels, the more of a tyrant he may become. He attempts to mask his fear and humiliation with a take-charge attitude that usually results in unquestioned intimidation. His wife, fearing his anger, becomes more passive, hiding behind the facade of a "supportive, submissive wife."

One of my favorite stories is the one told in the Broadway musical *The King and I* and the motion picture *Anna and the King*. Anna, a British widow, is sent to the small Eastern country of Siam. The King of Siam has absolute authority. He is a dictator. His country and all of his servants expect him to make wise decisions for them without question. The story tells of the King's loneliness that Anna is able to touch. Although as a woman she is under his authority, he begins to rely on her unique perspective, her knowledge of the world and her concern for him. Instead of being a threat, Anna gives the king great comfort in her strength and counsel.

The King of Siam had the opportunity for absolute authority. This position led him to misery, confusion, anxiety and loneliness. He gladly relinquished his need to "know it all" when he developed a trusting relationship with a strong, influential but submissive woman. Although many husbands may outwardly fight for absolute power, life as a dictator will destroy them. Absolute power leads to exploitation, fear and, ultimately, isolation. Appropriate submission leads to greater trust and greater intimacy.

So What Exactly Is Submission?

Now that we have established what it does *not* mean, let's look at what submission actually means. The word that appears as "submission" in English is a translation of the Greek word *hupotasso*. In the Greek language, this word means "a voluntary attitude of giving in and cooperating." When a woman submits, she places herself under the authority of another. A wife is commanded to willingly recognize her husband's leadership role within the home and to respond in deference. Submission calls for a woman to use her power in a way that will not challenge, dominate or undermine her husband's authority, but which instead will support it. The word submit was often used in the Greek culture as a military term. It communicated the idea, once again, of voluntarily placing oneself under the direct authority of another for the purpose of a higher goal.

Wives are not the only ones who are called to submit in scripture. Christians are commanded to submit to each other (I Corinthians 16:15 and Ephesians 5:21), to church leaders (Hebrews 2:13) and to government (Romans 13:1 and I Peter 2:13). In each of these cases, adults willingly recognize another's place of authority.

It is very difficult to understand how God intended the power and influence He has given to wives to be used within the spirit of submission. It is so easy to misunderstand submission as the absence of power and influence. Many women believe that they are submitting by adopting the attitude of, "Whatever he does is fine. I will just follow along." Then they feel abandoned, violated and resentful when their husbands lead their family into financial, emotional or moral ruin.

A submissive woman does not abandon her influence in her marriage. In fact, she accentuates it. The more influence she has with her husband, the better. She wants him to know her thoughts, feelings and opinions. She wants to be his confidante, the one he turns to in good and bad times. One of the best words to describe the spirit of submission is "empower." To empower means "to promote the self-actualization or influence of." In essence, a woman empowers her husband when she uses her influence and strength to help him to become a stronger, more confident and godly person. Instead of threatening his influence, her power actually heightens it. She adds to his strength and abilities rather than challenging them.

The opposite of a submissive woman is a dominant woman. This distinction is made not because one uses her power and the other does not, rather because each one uses her influence for exactly opposite reasons. The dominant woman cannot trust her husband's leadership. So she uses all of her influence to take his power away from him. Her desire is to make all of the decisions herself, even if she makes them through him. She invests all of her energy into convincing him that she is more capable than he is. When he disagrees with her, she says in anger, "Suit yourself. Just see what kind of a mess you get into when you don't have me to help you." Every time he fails, she reminds him, "I told you not to do that. If you would only listen to me . . . !" Over time, her husband becomes weaker, more insecure and less in touch with how to meet his family's needs.

The dominant wife's motives may not be evil. In most

cases, she is not a conniving wench driven to turn her husband into a weeping mess. In fact, she is likely responding to the inevitable situations in which he has let her down. She has convinced herself that she cannot trust him—and she has evidence to support her case. However, the more she dominates him, the less of a capable leader he becomes.

On the other hand, the submissive wife uses all of her God-given influence to build her husband's ability to lead. She presents her ideas, opinions and feelings in a way that builds his confidence and adds to his ability to understand his family's needs. Her goal is not to take his leadership away, but to empower him daily to grow into this difficult role. She does not use his mistakes to prove his inadequacies, but she succeeds and fails with him. She convinces him that she believes in him and will be by his side. She is able to wait for his leadership, even if she believes that she could do a better job. She tells him daily, through her trust, that she needs him to be a strong and capable leader. Her goal is to convince him that he can trust her with everything he is. The message that her submission communicates is: "I know you are not perfect, but I trust in your love. I believe you are capable of being the great leader for our family that God has called you to be. I will help you with all that I am to achieve this goal, even if at times my love hurts you. I will not expect you to be more than you are or allow you to be less than you are."

What an inspiring message for a woman to give her husband every day of his life! Over time, the strength that she gives will inevitably empower her husband to grow. The beginning of intimacy is really accepting the *mission* of submission. When a wife embraces the goal of communicating this attitude, it will change the way she views every decision, every conflict and each interaction with her husband. It is no longer "I win, you lose," but "I can't win unless I am helping you win."

Let's Get Practical

What does submission look like in real life? How does a woman take the high ideals of submission and apply them to paying the bills, raising kids and keeping the toilet seat down? Each marriage has its own personality. Every couple has certain things they fight about, unique ways of expressing love and very different life circumstances. However, there are some universal principles that can help all women submit in a way that will promote growth and intimacy in their marriages.

He Has Veto Power

Both my mom and dad are very strong people with definite opinions. My mom is a wonderful example of a wife who has used her influence and power to strengthen my dad's ability to lead. In most cases, my parents agreed on the major issues of life, including raising six children. However, there were exceptions. As every couple inevitably does, they ran into a difficult decision that they absolutely disagreed on. My dad wanted to move to Florida and my mom did not. After months and months of debating, struggling and praying, they had to make a decision—to move or not to move. This is when a husband's leadership is key. My mom still wanted to stay in Ohio, but she submitted to her husband's veto power, and they moved to Florida. Whether their life would have been happier in either place is not the issue. Even though my mother relinquished her desire to stay in Ohio, she recognized the importance of building something more important—a strong relationship with my father, regardless of where they lived.

In marriage, a husband has 51 percent of the stock. He casts the deciding vote. Once again, this does not mean that he will impulsively cast all of his votes. If he is wise, he will prayerfully consider the opinions and welfare of his wife. But at the end of the day, he makes the decision.

I can remember one day being faced with the choice of giving Mike veto power in a disagreement. We had not been married long and were having a friend over for dinner. Mike and I had been faithful to always pray together before meals. However, our friend was not a Christian and never prayed before eating his meals. Before our friend arrived, Mike told me not to wait to say a prayer before eating. He did not want to offend his friend by praying. I disagreed. I told Mike that this was our house and that we should honor God through our faithfulness. How could we ever share faith with our friend if we did not demonstrate our faithfulness?

After several minutes of sharing our respective opinions, we still could not agree. I finally said to Mike through gritted teeth, "You know how I feel. But you are the head of the house and I trust you to make the right decision." Our friend then arrived for lunch. We sat down at the table and the moment of truth arrived. Mike picked up his fork to signal that he was not going to pray. Amazingly, our friend looked at Mike and said,

"Aren't we going to pray before we eat?" Mike and I later laughed knowing that God had worked the situation out in His own way. Although this example is a rather insignificant event, it reminds me that the Lord will honor the faithfulness of a wife who is willing to trust His design for marriage. I had trusted His design for marriage by relinquishing control.

Never Exploit His Vulnerability

A wife knows better than anyone in the world how to get her way with her husband. She is aware of her husband's weak spots and knows exactly what buttons to push to get him to respond to her. What a wife does with her husband's vulnerabilities is very telling of whether or not she is truly committed to an attitude of submission.

There is no easier way to take control from your husband than to exploit his vulnerability. One humorous quote from Mark Twain explains: "Clothes make the man. A naked man has very little influence." In some respects, a wife can make her husband feel completely naked and without protection. He can never be an effective leader for their family when he is wallowing in his own failure and vulnerability.

Ron feels very inadequate about his work. He is a manual laborer who gets paid little more than minimum wage. His wife, Carol, knows how insecure he feels in this area. If she makes even the slightest comment related to earning potential, Ron feels defeated. Carol has a choice to make. She holds in her hand a very powerful trump card. If she really wants to challenge Ron on something, all she has to do is use it. However, if Carol is committed to submission, she knows that exploiting Ron's insecurity will eventually erode his confidence. She commits herself to encouraging him in this area. Every day, she thanks him for working hard for his family. If he brings up his modest wages, she reminds him that she would rather have him than a castle full of gold. She uses her strength to build his confidence.

This is a difficult task. You want to make right decisions for yourself and your family. There are times when your husband will mess up. Sometimes this happens because he did not take your advice. *Supporting him means that you have to let go of always making the right decision and focus on building the right relationship!*

Always Use the Language of Oneness

Coaches often say, "There is no I in TEAM." In relationships, there is always a place for individuality. For example, good communication begins with sentences that start with "I think . . ." and "I feel . . ." However, marriage is made up of two individuals who are joined together for a common journey. Regardless of the outcome, making decisions in the spirit of oneness is vital.

I recently met with a couple who had some very difficult decisions to make. After listening to each opinion and perspective, I responded: "What you decide is less important than how you come to that decision. Neither of your perspectives is superior, and things will likely be okay regardless of what you decide. It is the fighting, arguing and blaming that may occur while making the decision that can ultimately create harm."

Couples can cope with almost any situation as long as they

believe that they are in it together; but when it becomes "my opinion versus yours," the blaming starts and oneness stops. There is a time to express individual thoughts, feelings and preferences; and then there is a time to make decisions as a united couple.

A common example of this is in parenting. Naturally, a husband and wife will often disagree on how to raise their children. One may be stricter and one more lenient. One trusts their sixteen-year-old to drive, the other does not. Good parents spend time talking through these differences. Eventually, they decide how to respond to a problem. Then, both mom and dad communicate to their children, "We have decided . . ."

The temptation of a wife is to remind her husband in hindsight how much better her opinion was than his. "If you only would have listened to me!" or "Aren't you glad you took my advice?" No matter what happens, a wife is submissive when she uses the word we. "That's okay. We've gotten out of bigger jams!" "We can handle this together." "I'm really glad we decided to do this." We language communicates, "I trust your leadership for our team."

Taking the Plunge

"I am a loud, opinionated person!" a woman once told me. "It may be easy for you to have a 'submissive and quiet spirit,' but it is impossible for me!" It is easy to think of a submissive woman as one who is always respectful, ladylike, courteous and soft-spoken. Not so! A woman is not submissive because she is quiet and refined. No matter her personality, her spirit will either stubbornly seek her own way or willingly yield when submission is appropriate. Any woman can be submissive. In fact, scripture is clear that God's design for marriage is for all husbands and wives—not just for the ones who fit the mold. The command for a wife to submit is very clear in several New Testament passages:

Wives, submit to your husbands as to the Lord. For the husband is the head of the wife as Christ is the head of the church, his body, of which He is the Savior. Now as the church submits to Christ, so also wives should submit to their husbands in everything.

(Ephesians 5:22–24, NIV)

Wives, submit to your husbands, as is fitting in the Lord.

(Colossians 3:18, NIV)

Wives, in the same way be submissive to your husbands so that, if any of them do not believe the word, they may be won over without words by the behavior of their wives, when they see the purity and reverence of your lives.

(I Peter 3:1,2, NIV)

Along with each teaching on how a woman should relate to her husband is a command relating to how a husband should treat his wife. Invariably, scripture charges a husband to love and cherish his wife. If a husband is faithful to his role, submission in a Christian marriage is safe because a wife's interests and opinions will be valued. It would not be that hard to submit to a husband who acted like Prince Charming! Unfortunately, a wife's submission does not appear to be necessary only when her husband is loving.

The first passage listed on the previous page, Ephesians 5:24, says that a wife should submit to her husband *in everything*. This raises some very important questions. Is there ever a time when a wife should not submit? What should a woman do when her husband is abusing his authority? Examples of this include an abusive spouse, an alcoholic, an unbeliever, a husband who is financially irresponsible or a very controlling husband. Should a wife truly obey a man like this in everything?

Unfortunately, the Bible does not tackle these difficult questions for us in an obvious manner. In fact, the command to submit in everything seems to run totally against a loving God who wants to protect us from harmful and evil leadership. Would He really want an abused wife to stay in a relationship in which she was daily assaulted by her husband? Would He want children to continue to be sexually molested by their father as their mother clings to the role of submission?

Submission is not absolute. Each of these three scriptures also uses an important qualifier to the command of submission. Ephesians 5 says to submit "as to the Lord." Likewise, Colossians 3:18 says to submit "as is fitting to the Lord." In I Peter 3:6, Peter continues his discussion of submission telling women to "do what is right." God gives husbands authority within marriage. Wives defer to husbands out of reverence and obedience to God. It is not a husband's authority that ultimately rules, but God's.

Whenever a Christian is called to submit to a human authority (boss, husband, pastor, government, etc.), God is recognized as the larger authority. This means that when God's law is in conflict with a human authority, a Christian submits to God rather than man. For example, Roman authorities ordered that Paul and other Christians could not preach the Gospel. Paul continued to share the news of Jesus Christ because God had commanded him to "preach the Gospel."

How should Christian women deal with this conflict? Is the principle of submission only valid when a husband is behaving righteously? If this were the case, women would have daily excuses why submission does not apply to them. After all, husbands are human and make mistakes daily. These are very difficult questions that affect the daily life of every woman to some extent. How can a wife know when submission is appropriate and when to say "no?" The next chapter will address specific situations that call for a wise balance between power and submission.

As I have studied the biblical concept of submission, my attitude has slowly changed from reluctance to enthusiasm. I am learning that submission is a great challenge. My excitement comes from the realization that this is a role to which God has called me. Submission requires that I become the best that I can be, and use that strength to develop my trust in God rather than trying to get my way. This is how God can teach me to become more like Christ. The Lord has equipped me to use my power in a way that will not only promote growth in my husband, but will ultimately result in the intimacy that I long for—both within my marriage and in my relationship to God.

The wise woman builds her house, but with her own hands the foolish one tears hers down.

Proverbs 14:1, NIV

Questions for Discussion and Reflection

1. What is your gut reaction to the word "submission?"

2. Read Ephesians 5:22 and Colossians 3:18. What do the phrases "as to the Lord" and "as is fitting to the Lord" mean related to the command for a wife to submit to her husband?

3. Do you think God has your interest in mind when he commands wives to be submissive? Why or why not?

4. What misunderstandings of the concept of submission have you witnessed? How can these misconceptions lead to destruction in a marriage?

5. In your own words, what does it mean for you to submit to your husband? On a scale from one to ten, how willing are you to do this? What stands in your way?

6. What practical questions do you face in your marriage related to submission? How does the information presented in this chapter about what submission is and is not clarify those questions for you?

Four

How Did Our Kingdom Become a Dictatorship?

I gave up on intimacy years ago," Jill told me after attending a marriage conference. She described a stifled existence living with a controlling, dominant husband. There were no bars and no jumpsuits, but her home felt like a prison. Every move had to be approved by him; every dollar accounted for. Both Jill and the kids walked on eggshells, afraid to awaken the wrath of the "king" of the house.

Jill was shriveling under the absolute control of a husband who ruled with an iron hand. She could no longer tell whether her deference was out of fear or submission. With each passing day, her husband became "stronger" as Jill slipped further and further into the stance of a helpless victim. Her talents and skills, which at one time had flourished, withered without the warm rays of freedom and encouragement. She felt like a slave who obeyed orders and suppressed opinions, who was left with shattered dreams and seething anger. She knew that her children were suffering a worse fate than she was. As much as she tried to encourage them, the harsh words spoken by their father would leave irreparable damage. Surely God did not intend for submission to create this mess!

How did a woman like Jill get into such a stifling marriage? Certainly this was not the kind of existence she hoped for when she wed! One of the greatest mistakes that women make is allowing their husbands to assume the role of a dictator. It does not happen overnight. In fact, the process often begins during courtship. Infatuated by his love and looking for a powerful man, she lets him tell her what to do. He decides what friends she can see and how she spends her money. Then they get married. Slowly, his control spreads to all areas of their life together. Before she knows it, she feels trapped in his web of power and dominance.

There are two primary factors that promote dictatorships within marriage. First of all, some women fear their own influence and power. At some level, they are attracted to men who will take control of their lives. For these women, the dream of the prince is so strong that they would rather be "rescued" by a tyrant than have to fend for themselves.

Many times, such women have grown up in homes in which their opinions were not valued. They spent the first twenty years of life learning that they should be silent. They were never encouraged to develop their gifts, their talents or their "voice."

Although living in a dictatorship is unfulfilling, it feels strangely familiar and secure to these women. They have never dealt with their own potential nor abilities. Being without this "powerful" man is similar to being alone in a dark forest with no survival skills. Out of habit and fear, they always defer to him. Over time, their husbands believe the message that these women communicate daily: "I am worthless. My opinion does not count." At many levels, this has become a self-fulfilling prophecy.

The second factor that contributes to dictatorships is an improper understanding of submission. Many times, women who fear their own strength rely on the biblical teaching of submission to support their weak position in their marriages.

In the last chapter, we talked about the importance of submission. Clearly, God has designed the husband to be the head of the household. However, it is very important for women to understand that submission does not mean that wives surrender their influence. In fact, it takes a very strong and powerful woman to appropriately submit to her husband. Submission should never be used as an excuse to hide from the influence and responsibility that wives have within marriage.

There is a vast and distinct difference between a woman who is appropriately submissive and a woman who is just plain weak. This difference is communicated through two words: *empower* and *enable*.

Submission results in a wife empowering her husband. This means that all of her strength is behind him. She uses everything that she is and has to help him become an effective and capable leader. Her submission does not dominate him. She will not force him to make good decisions. However, she wisely uses her influence, lending him the strength he will need to become a godly man.

Weakness leads to a woman who enables her husband. When she enables him, she essentially allows the worst of him to emerge. She provides no strength, no accountability and no encouragement towards the right things. In fact, she may even help him to go down the wrong path by encouraging him to make bad decisions.

When Mike and I take road trips, he is usually the driver and I am the navigator. I have the maps and look for road signs, landmarks and speed traps. Getting to our destination always requires teamwork. It is also a wonderful metaphor for the concepts of empowering and enabling.

As a "submissive" wife, I sit in the passenger seat. I am just as capable of driving as Mike, but I yield that responsibility to him. If he gets tired during the trip, he may ask me to temporarily fill his role. My role as navigator is very important. He will need to make split-second decisions. "Do I get off at this exit?" "Which freeway do we take?" "What's the speed limit?" "Do the kids need to use the bathroom?" I have, at my fingertips, volumes of information that he needs in order to negotiate through the obstacles on our trip. I use all of my resources to *empower* him in his task.

But what if I thought I was too stupid to read a map or road signs? "I don't know! I'm not sure if I read the sign correctly! I forget. Which way is north?" If he were accidentally going the wrong way down a one-way street, what if I said to myself, "He'll figure it out. I just need to keep my mouth shut." What if I never told him that the kids needed to eat and use the bathroom? Our trip would be a disaster.

This is exactly how many women respond to their role of navigator in marriage. No wonder their families never reach their destination!

A large aspect of a wife's role is understanding when she may be enabling her husband to become a poor leader. Of course, she should never use her influence to dominate him. However, she should also not use her influence to support foolishness or ungodliness.

There Is a Time to Say "No"

Perhaps the most difficult question I have ever wrestled with is this: *When is it appropriate for a woman to say "no" to her husband? When should she refuse to submit?* As a counselor, I have encountered many women who are in desperate situations. Their plights come in all different presentations: husbands who abuse them or their children, use pornography, deny them freedom, refuse to work . . . the list goes on and on.

Many of these women unwittingly contribute to these problems by their inaction. Their husbands are clearly going the wrong way down a one-way street. They sit in the passenger seat, fearing what may happen to them and their children. But still, they say nothing. As he continues to drive to certain death, these women keep themselves and their children in the car, often paralyzed by fear.

The Old Testament story of Abigail is an illustration of a wife who rightly refused to follow her husband's immoral leadership. The Bible describes Abigail as a "sensible and beautiful woman" who was married to Nabel. According to scripture, Nabel was "surly and mean in his dealings" (I Samuel 25:3, NIV).

While wandering around, avoiding Saul, David came across a large group of shepherds who worked for Nabel. David and the men that were with him helped protect Nabel's shepherds for a time. When David and his men were ready to leave the area, he sent a messenger to Nabel asking for some food and provisions in return for their work. Nabel insulted David and refused to give him anything. When David got the news, he was furious. He commanded his men to destroy Nabel and his family.

When Abigail heard about what had happened, she rushed to David with gifts and kindness. She accepted responsibility for Nabel's actions, and pleaded with David not to act impulsively. She persuaded him not to kill Nabel. The Lord dealt with Nabel, killing him just days later. Abigail eventually became David's wife.

Abigail was not submissive to her husband in this story. She went against Nabel's orders by giving David gifts and food. She acted in this way because her husband was behaving in a foolish manner that almost lead to the death of their whole family. Abigail not only assumed the leadership of her family at this point, but she was also very influential to David in a respectful manner. She helped him calm down and prevented him from impulsively murdering Nabel.

Abigail's was clearly a situation in which her husband's leadership would have destroyed their family had she not intervened. In some marriages, this is the case. When drastic perversions of leadership occur—like abuse, addiction and gross immorality—a godly woman must temporarily take "the driver's seat" in order to prevent the calamity.

Unfortunately, many decisions about submission are less clear. I have gained tremendous respect for women who honestly grapple with this delicate matter in their own lives. They seek to serve God and plead for clear direction in difficult circumstances. They want neither their children nor their husbands to be destroyed by their actions. They walk the fine line of strength and submission.

It is imperative that wives resist supporting foolish or tyrannical leadership that risks dreadful consequences. There are no obvious answers for women in this situation. However, applying the following principles may provide direction.

A Wife Should Not Behave in a Sinful Manner, Even if Her Husband Tells Her To

If a husband demands that his wife behave in an ungodly manner, she should not submit to his authority. Rather, she should submit to God's. Romans 13 talks about submitting to the government. Paul writes ". . . there is no authority except that which God has established" (Romans 13:1, NIV). God gives a husband's authority to him and he is under God's authority. When a husband asks his wife to do something that is clearly sinful, God vetoes his authority.

If a husband asks his wife to be involved in sexually immoral behaviors like watching a pornographic movie, she should refuse his proposal. If he tells her to lie, she should not. If he forbids that she go to church or if he tells her to treat her parents in a dishonorable way, she must not submit.

If you hire a babysitter to watch your children, you expect your kids to listen to what she says. In fact, you may tell them, "Whatever Sandy tells you to do, you obey her." Imagine that Sandy tells the kids to run through the streets naked in the middle of winter. Would you want your kids to obey her? Of course not. In fact, you would be proud of them if they said, "Our mother would never want us to do that. I am calling her." That babysitter has authority only because you have given it to her. Her job is to follow the spirit of your parenting. If she does not do that, then you take authority away from her.

When your kids reach a certain age, you expect them to thoughtfully apply what they know about the rules to what other authorities (such as coaches, babysitters and teachers) tell them to do. In some cases, you expect them to refuse to obey. God expects us to do this with those He has placed in authority over us.

God holds women responsible who act sinfully, even under the leadership of their husbands. Acts 5 tells the story of a husband and wife who were co-conspirators in sin. Ananias and his wife, Sapphira, sold a piece of land and promised to give the proceeds to the church. They secretly decided to hold some of the money back.

Although there was nothing wrong with keeping some of the money, they lied to their church. First, Ananias told Peter that they had donated the full amount to the church. God killed Ananias on the spot.

About three hours later, Sapphira came to Peter. She had no idea what had just happened to her husband. She was, however, party to his deception. Peter asked her, "Tell me, is this the price you and Ananias got for the land?" And she said, "Yes, that is the price" (Acts 5:8, NIV). Sapphira was then delivered the same fate that her husband had just faced.

In this story, God dealt equally with this husband and wife. They made the decision to sin together, and each was given the opportunity to come clean. Sapphira was punished harshly for her sin, even though she was acting in "submission" to her husband.

A Wife Should Protect the Dignity of All in Her Household

Much is said today about defending your own rights. The rights of individuals are protected above all else. In fact, people seem to have the right to everything: free speech, independent thought, a job, food, medical care, access to guns, sexual expression—the list goes on. Recently, an incident was reported of a woman who was attending a professional basketball game. The team mascot approached her during the halftime show and coaxed her to dance on the floor with him. The woman later sued the basketball team for violating her right of privacy!

Perhaps our society has taken the idea of individual rights to an extreme. However, the concept of personal rights did not originate with the American Civil Liberties Union. Scripture is very clear about the value and dignity of each human being.

Men and women are separate from all creation in that they were created in God's image. Their souls are eternal, they are able to make moral decisions and they are deeply sensitive to interactions with others.

Based on the value that God has given to humans, we are commanded to treat each other with love and kindness (I Peter 3:8). Regardless of one's age, wealth, race, gender or position in society, this status as an image-bearer of God makes each person precious.

Although Jesus understood the weakness and sinfulness of man, he treated people with great respect. Sometimes his dealings with them were harsh, but "tough love" was still in the spirit of restoring their souls. This has implications not only for the way we treat others, but also for the way that we allow ourselves and others to be treated.

Jesus was a strong champion of the dignity of others. He particularly defended the value of those who were trampled upon by society (the poor, the sick, children, widows, tax collectors). One of the most beautiful examples of this is the account in John 8 of a woman who was caught in adultery. She was dragged through the city streets and about to be stoned by the religious leaders. He said to her accusers, "If any one of you is without sin, let him be the first to throw a stone at her." After the men had all left, Jesus said to the woman, "Neither do I condemn you; Go now and leave your life of sin" (John 8:3–11, NIV).

Fathers, in particular, are placed in the role of protecting their children. This does not only include physical protection, but also emotional and spiritual protection. Instead, a man can use his strength and position of authority to devastate his children. You may know personally the lasting effects of a father who communicated to you that you were worthless. Adults carry around in their minds vivid memories of hurtful words like, "You are a failure. I curse the day you were born. You are so stupid, you'll never amount to anything." When a man abuses his position of power and authority to communicate such destructive messages, his wife must step in to protect and reaffirm the dignity of those in her home.

Becoming the defender of a child is a natural thing. Even animals will fight to the death to protect their children. However, many women are simply confused about how to react when the threat to a child comes from within their own home. Their fear of confrontation and anger may keep them silent when they know what is happening is wrong. Defending a child from an angry or abusive spouse can still be done in the spirit of respect. It requires clearly and strongly communicating, "This behavior is harmful and I won't let it occur in our home."

The thought of defending their own dignity may be a little more difficult for some women. The New Testament talks quite a bit about placing oneself in the position of a servant. Christians are often encouraged to voluntarily lay down their rights and to minister to others. Christ is used as an example of this in Philippians 2:5–9. Christian women often use such scripture verses to justify putting themselves in the position of a victim. However, being a servant and being a doormat are two different things.

Proverbs 31 depicts a woman described as an "excellent"

wife. Every Mother's Day, thousands of sermons use her life as the example that women strive to emulate. Certainly, she was a defender and provider of the poor, her servants and her children. Yet while serving others, she also retained a sense of her own value. Proverbs 31:25 says, "She is clothed with strength and dignity."

There is a very important distinction between serving others and allowing others to walk all over your dignity. Let's say that I decide to work at a soup kitchen to help feed those who are less fortunate than I am. In doing this, I voluntarily give of my time and of myself to serve others and to serve God. While walking to back to my car, I am approached by a man to whom I have just served a meal. This man has a gun and is threatening to assault me. Should I do what he says in the name of serving him? Of course not! I should do everything within my power to protect myself, and him, from this degrading behavior. There is a tremendous difference between serving him food and allowing him to violate me.

A similar dynamic occurs in some marriages. A husband, through abuse of his leadership position, may behave in a way that degrades his wife. He may humiliate her emotionally, socially and sexually. By doing this, he is robbing her of the worth and dignity with which she was created. Allowing this to occur should never be confused with servanthood or submission.

Over the past several years, there has been a rash of church vandalism. Newspapers worldwide report incidents of people burning and vandalizing churches. In many cases, vandals paint obscene words and symbols on the walls and furniture.

As Christians, this enrages us. We are disgusted by the disrespect that someone would show to a house of God. Were it within our power, certainly we would do whatever possible to stop such atrocities. A church is only a building. Scripture teaches that, as Christians, we are the temple of the Holy Spirit (II Corinthians 6:16). Yet, in the spirit of submission, shall we allow someone to rip apart and vandalize our minds, souls and bodies?

Refusal to submit, in this case, does not suggest that women go on the attack when their dignity is compromised in marriage. Too often, the natural reaction to humiliation is to retaliate. Perhaps he says, "You are absolutely worthless! Your cooking stinks, the house is a mess and you are still earning minimum wage. You should thank your lucky stars that I stay with you." Then she says, "The only reason I'm stuck in this trap is because I married you. If you would start earning a decent living for once, I might be able to go back to school!"

Although retaliation is an easy trap to fall into, it only makes matters worse. Defending your dignity simply means refusing to allow such an interchange to occur. For example, in the middle of an argument a man says to his wife, "Your ideas are so stupid, I don't even know why I ever listen to you." The wife replies, "That is an unfair statement, and I'm not going to talk about this any more until you can be respectful."

This is much easier said than done. Defending your dignity is difficult to do, even in a benign situation. Standing up for yourself or for someone else may seem almost impossible in a relationship rife with fear and intimidation. (The book *Boundaries,* by Henry Cloud and John Townsend, is a good resource for women who have difficulty discerning when it is appropriate to stand up for themselves. It also provides helpful examples of how this can be done in a variety of situations.)

A thirty-eight-year-old woman named Holly came to counseling for help in her abusive marriage. At first she was vague about the problems she was having. She talked about feeling depressed and anxious all of the time. She played down the troubles in her marriage, saying that her husband was basically a good guy who sometimes made mistakes. After a few months, she began to share the fear that she felt at home. Although she resisted calling it abuse, she described how her husband occasionally became hostile and violent with her.

Deep down, Holly felt responsible for the problems in her marriage. She tried desperately to please her husband and avoid his raging fits. She felt that she must deserve her misery for mistakes she had made in the past. Every fiber of her being seemed to fight the realization that she was in an abusive and dangerous marriage.

There are many women like Holly, who quietly endure living with threatening men. Others are married to lesser versions of abusive husbands. Although the degree of their terror varies, women who live in dictatorships share a dream that has turned into a nightmare. For several reasons, it is often difficult for them to accept the peril of their situation. They are too afraid, humiliated and often isolated to seek help. The nightmare lives on, often justified by a facade of submission, humility and meekness.

Saying "no" in an abusive relationship is very difficult. The fear can be paralyzing. The most important thing to do is to seek help—a trusted friend, a pastor, a counselor or a relative. As difficult as it may be to take the first step, allowing such behavior to continue is a tragic mistake.

A Wife Should Not Enable Her Husband to Live in Sin

This principle is a little more tricky. A wife should not try to *control* the conduct of her husband. However, she does play an active role in *responding* to his behavior. As described in chapter two, a wife has a lot of influence with her husband. He looks for her support and approval in whatever he is doing. She must not use this influence to encourage behavior that is sinful. She should not ignore his sin, nor should she provide for it to continue.

A good example of this is an alcoholic husband. In order for his alcoholism to continue, devastating their home, his wife must in some ways support it. She may look the other way and even help keep his drinking a secret. She covers for him when he cannot make it to work, makes excuses for him with his friends and family and compensates for his lack of involvement in the home. She may even do this with the intention of being submissive. In order for their marriage to heal, she must confront his addiction and refuse to play a supportive role in his destructive pattern.

If a wife supports her husband's sinful lifestyle, the natural consequences will likely be debilitating for their entire family. Joshua 7 tells a story illustrating the destruction that enabling sin can bring about. The Israelites had just defeated a pagan country. God told them they should destroy everything they found in the country. Aachan, an Israelite, buried some gold under the floor of his tent. His family, living in the tent, was obviously aware of his act. A very weak country then defeated the Israelites. When Joshua prayed, God revealed to him that someone had taken gold from the pagan country. All of the Israelites were told that a search would be conducted. Aachan's sin was revealed. God commanded the Israelites to stone Aachan's entire family.

In modern-day America, God usually does not punish sin as quickly as he did with the Israelites. However, sin does have serious emotional, spiritual and physical consequences. Those consequences are not just for the sinner, but also for those related to the sinner. The impact of sexual abuse, for example, is felt by anyone involved with the perpetrator.

For most women, the natural way of trying to influence a husband is to nag. "Harry, don't you think you've had enough to drink?" "Tom, I've asked you a hundred times to pay the bills!" "I wish you would stop swearing in front of the kids!"

This strategy has been proven over the centuries to do one thing: backfire. The more a woman nags, the less a man listens. If a man is addicted to pornography, the last thing that will motivate him to stop is his wife's constant nagging. It would be humiliating for him to change his life just because she told him to. In fact, he may even become more involved in it to prove to his wife that she cannot control him. This does *not* mean that she has no influence over his behavior. Her influence may come in a rather paradoxical way.

In I Peter 3, Peter tells wives to influence their husbands through a "gentle and quiet spirit." It is through a wife's consistent strength, which may be quietly manifested, that she speaks the loudest to the man she loves.

A wife's ultimate goal is to help her husband clearly see the destructive choices he is making. For example, through pornography, he is alienating himself from his wife emotionally, sexually and spiritually. He is also distancing himself from God and other Christians. She must be sure that she does not protect him from experiencing this alienation. Instead of pouting and pleading, she should firmly state that she cannot be sexually intimate with him, while he is involved with sexual immorality. Enough said. Then she consistently, prayerfully and quietly follows through.

When a woman uses her influence this way, her husband is clearly placed in the role of making his own decision. He cannot blame her for his lifestyle. She takes herself out of the equation. He becomes fully aware of the consequences of whatever he chooses. The responsibility for action becomes his.

Although very important, a wife's influence is limited. Even if she says and does everything right, her husband may still continue with this destructive lifestyle. Her job is not to change him. Ultimately, his moral decisions are between him and God. Understanding the power of a wife's influence and the boundary of her responsibility is a delicate balance to achieve. Although she cannot force her husband to act a certain way, she can influence him. She can refuse to be a party to his sinful choices, be a consistent testimony through the purity of her own life and pray for him.

James Dobson's classic book, *Love Must Be Tough,* is a wonderful explanation of how a wife can wisely influence her husband who is going astray. It seems a lot more direct to nag, beg and plead for him to change. The more desperate a wife feels, the more she has to resist trying to "fix" her husband. She can only influence him through her strength. Never through desperation.

In extreme cases of sinful leadership in a family, a wife should separate from her husband. The separation should be for the purpose of biblical discipline and restoring him to godliness. In the case of abuse, a woman and children must be removed from the home for the purpose of their safety. Once again, the wife is not submitting to her husband, she is submitting to God through the church. In cases of sexual immorality, scripture also provides for divorce. Whenever possible, church elders and pastors should be party to the separation and divorce. Church officials often serve as mediators, counselors and sources of support and accountability. For many husbands and wives, the involvement of their church has made a tremendous difference.

For the wife of a Christian, the church serves as a form of accountability for her husband. A Christian marriage is performed by an ordained minister as a sign that it is under the church's authority.

Obviously, for a husband who is not a Christian, the authority of the church has very little influence. For an unbelieving husband, the state provides accountability. In fact, all marriages are under the authority of the government. Remember what the minister or justice of the peace said at the end of your wedding? "By the authority granted to me by the state of ___, I now pronounce you man and wife." Domestic judges grant protection to a spouse or children who are in harmful situations in their family (restraining orders, legal separations, divorce, etc.).

There are several authorities that are greater than a husband's. The most important, of course, is God's. When a wife finds herself unable to support the leadership of her husband, this does not leave her alone in the wilderness. She is still, as always, under the sovereign protection and guidance of God.

This concept gives women great hope. God did not intend for a wife to be solely at the mercy of a "toxic" husband. A Christian wife hopes in God and in his ultimate authority.

There are times when government leaders make decisions that are immoral and unethical. I cringe when I think of the impact godless leaders have on the country that my children will inherit. Then I remember that I am not *ultimately* under the authority or the protection of the government. God is in control! If I am faithful, He will protect me when our country's leaders fail. It may not be easy or fun, but I am in His hands.

I am also responsible to use the vehicles I have to help keep the government accountable to God's authority. I can vote for men and women who uphold wisdom and morality. I can express my opinion when I disagree with the current leadership. The time may even come for civil disobedience if the government's laws contradict God's.

The same holds true for women who find themselves under the authority of a man who is morally or emotionally incapable of good leadership. If the day comes when submission to a husband is no longer appropriate, it is not replaced by dominating.

It is replaced by submission to God, through the church.

Many who live in dictatorships feel helpless to bring about change. Dictatorships are designed to limit the power of everyone, except the assumed ruler. It is often through fear and intimidation that a wife becomes convinced that she has no say in her marriage. But it is the perfect love of Christ that casts out all fear. She must not abandon the role to which God has called her. He will give her the strength she needs.

Relying on the strength of God can also help a woman understand that tyranny is truly a sign of weakness. The dominance of a dictator is not strength. It results instead from insecurity and fear. This is demonstrated in *Beauty and the Beast,* the classic fairy tale recently retold in an animated Disney movie and a stage production. A ferocious and ugly beast captures Belle, the beautiful, cheerful and loyal young maiden. Locked in the Beast's palace, Belle is totally under his tyranny. He makes unsuccessful efforts to win her affection through his gruff and intimidating commands. "You WILL come to dinner with me tonight!" he roars.

As the story progresses, it is clear that the Beast feels as weak and miserable as Belle does. His history of rejection and loss have made him a bitter and lonely creature, one who could not let himself be touched by the love of another. The only way a beast has of controlling his own fear is creating greater fear in those around him.

So what does *Beauty and the Beast* have to do with real life? Many women, like Belle, are locked in the castle with a "beast." Is that all he is? Is there a man to be found underneath all of that hostility and dominance?

Through Belle's strong and loving influence, the Beast was able to experience love. He felt safe enough to put aside his domineering and abusive ways. For many wives, there is hope for a happy ending to their dismal fairy tale of tyranny. Through applying wisdom and God's intervention, they may someday sow the seeds of intimacy in their marriage.

Unfortunately, there are also some beasts that cannot be tamed. Beyond a doubt, some women reading this book have husbands who may never abandon their dominating or abusive ways. These women may have surrendered the hope for intimacy long ago. Perhaps they simply long for the day when home is a safe haven.

The integrity of marriage is extremely important. However, fostering a relationship that threatens someone's safety and dignity defies the very spirit of marriage. If you live in a dictatorship, I implore you to seek wisdom and help. Please resist the temptation to misuse biblical concepts like submission or humility to justify a sinful and destructive pattern in marriage. Your husband is not the enemy. The real enemy is the fear that seizes both of you.

The wise woman builds her house, but with her own hands the foolish one tears hers down.

Proverbs 14:1, NIV

Questions for Discussion and Reflection

1. Do you think God designed marriage to result in a male dictatorship? Why or why not?

2. How might a misconception of submission result in a dictatorship? How does a true understanding of a wife's role in marriage (including submission) prevent a dictatorship?

3. What is the difference between a weak woman and a submissive woman? What is the difference between empowering your husband and enabling him?

4. According to this chapter, what are the three cases in which a wife should say "no?" What are the biblical arguments behind these three scenarios?

5. What practical steps should a woman take if she finds herself in a dictatorship?

Five

Nobody Told Me
That Marriage Could
Be So Lonely

I've tried everything I know and nothing has worked!" Helen exclaimed in frustration. "He seems content having the same old surface conversations day after day, year after year. I guess I'm the only one in this marriage who needs intimacy."

Echoes of Helen's complaints can be heard in counseling rooms, kitchens, telephone conversations, fellowship halls and walkways throughout the world. For as long as men and women have attempted marriage, the disparity between their expectations has existed. Intimacy. Women will do almost anything to experience it with a man. They flock to seminars, bookstores and informal meetings to learn how to "trick" their husbands into it. Men react to the idea of intimacy with all the excitement of a trip to the dentist. As the saying goes, "women give sex to get intimacy, and men give intimacy to get sex."

Are women the only ones who truly need intimacy in marriage? Are husbands really satisfied with cohabitation as long as there are weekly conjugal visits? If not, why do women seem to be the only ones driving for something deeper, something more meaningful?

Husbands Need Intimacy, Too

Sure, he appears to be happy watching the six o'clock news and glued to ESPN on the weekends. For him, a satisfying conversation may be talking about the construction on Interstate 95. Although it may seem that husbands will do anything to avoid the "I" word, men need intimacy as much as women do. In fact, they crave it! As crazy as it sounds, they often run from it and seek it at the same time. Why is a husband's approach to the concept of intimate conversations and emotional connection often one of fear?

John Gray, the author of the bestselling book, *Men Are From Mars, Women Are From Venus,* has been enormously successful in the amusing way he explains what we have known all along—men and women are different! As much as they have in common, the dissimilarities between a husband and a wife often make it seem as if they are coexisting aliens from different planets. The gender gap can be all but eliminated in most casual settings. However, in marriage all of the defenses are stripped away and raw humanity, male and female, is inevitably exposed.

One foundational difference is that men tend to be more focused on mastering their world and achieving goals, while women are more oriented toward relationships. In Genesis 3, God's responses to Adam and Eve after the Fall were very different. Adam's curse was directly related to his work. Eve's curse involved her family relationships.

From the time they learn to speak, girls are encouraged to practice relating to others, while boys learn to master and organize. Boys in the schoolyard are encouraged to become bigger than their pain. Girls cry and talk through their feelings. As a result of intuition and years of practice, women, on the whole, are better at relationships. Men, on the other hand, are not oriented toward developing and sustaining relationships. A deep friendship for a man is often seen as a luxury rather than a necessity.

This difference between husbands and wives is glaringly obvious when the couple seeks help in counseling. Tearfully, the wife makes the call, desperate for more in her marriage. "Why can't he understand how much his apathy hurts me? All I ask for is a little sensitivity!" she laments. "Please teach him how to love me."

Eventually, the wife manages to drag her husband in for the dreaded marriage therapy. He is reluctant, skeptical and defensive. Counseling is the last place on earth he wants to be. Once he begins talking, however, he complains about being picked on, nagged, scapegoated and compared to the "perfect" husband next door. He states his case that the "beautiful" girl he fell in love with has turned into the contentious woman that Solomon likens to constant dripping on a day of steady rain. "Why does she have to take everything so personally? Can't she just give me some space!"

The stereotypes of men and women are endless, but generally true. Many comedians have made a living by tapping into the delicate intricacies of married life. The sitcom *Home Improvement* is an excellent example of this. Tim "the Toolman" Taylor is a humorous caricature of the typical husband with his endless projects, macho mannerisms and amusing attempts at understanding his wife.

Everyone can relate to the basic differences between the normal husband and wife. She wants to talk about feelings. He wants just the facts. She longs for a big anniversary celebration. He would be happy with pizza and a movie. She wants to hear the symphony. He wants to watch the World Series. The list goes on and on.

A woman's greater tendency toward relationships and emotions does not mean that only females need intimacy. Although they may not gravitate toward it, men need intimacy too. Look at it this way: It is generally accepted that men are achievement-oriented. This drives their ability to provide financially for their families. Because most women are not naturally as achievement-oriented, does this mean that they don't need food, shelter or other material provisions? Certainly not! God has created the husband to be primarily oriented toward providing for the family's physical needs. In the same way, God has oriented the wife to be the primary force for meeting both of their needs for intimacy.

What would happen if you just gave up on trying to establish a relationship with your husband? In many cases, the relationship would just die. Your drive for closeness is important not just to make sure that your emotional needs are met. It also ensures that your husband stays connected.

By the Way, What Is Intimacy?

Intimacy. It is a word we throw around all of the time. As much as we use it, do we really know what it means to experience intimacy?

The word *intimate* comes from a Latin word that means "innermost." The concept of intimacy has three important aspects. It involves more than one person (two for our purpose). Both must disclose themselves, therefore, both must become vulnerable.

First of all, a person cannot be intimate with himself. A term like "individual intimacy" makes no sense. The purpose and format of intimacy is relationships—to be close to another person. This may seem obvious, but it is key to understanding the frustration some experience. In many relationships, only one person is actively interested in intimacy. Unless both become open to achieving an intimate relationship, it cannot occur. This also means that intimacy cannot be forced.

"Why won't you talk to me?" a woman asks her husband. The more a wife begs for intimacy, the more her husband may seem to avoid it. Intimacy requires two individuals who willingly seek it. As many women know, pleading and begging for intimacy in marriage can feel as futile as convincing an ATM machine to give you money.

FINALLY LORI FOUND OUT HOW TO GET HER HUSBAND'S ATTENTION

©2001 Julie Anderson.

Inherent in the process of becoming intimate, both individuals must work toward sharing themselves. In physical intimacy, people take off their clothes to allow for maximum closeness. In our society, disrobing is appropriate only in the context of trust and familiarity. Most people are comfortable taking off their coat or jacket in public. In front of friends, they may even kick off their shoes. However, only in the context of physical intimacy does someone bare their body for their partner to study and enjoy. In the same way, most people are willing to share a certain amount of themselves with casual acquaintances. Neighbors generally know each other's names, occupations and hobbies. Friends and family may know quite a bit about each other's histories, plans and concerns. However, people share their deepest thoughts, feelings and fears with only one or two others, if they ever share at all.

To become emotionally intimate they must be willing to remove their defenses and masks, baring their emotions for scrutiny and interaction. Like physical intimacy, true emotional closeness requires that both individuals be involved in sharing.

The third aspect of intimacy is that it inevitably leads to a state of vulnerability. When a man shares his innermost hopes and fears, he becomes relatively defenseless. When a woman communicates how she feels and what she longs for, she becomes open to rejection and hurt. There is no way to avoid the risk that inherently comes with intimacy. To achieve ultimate intimacy means to risk ultimate vulnerability. Although men and women desperately want and need intimacy, many are too afraid of the hurt to strive for closeness.

It Is Better to Be Safe Than Close

The concept of vulnerability helps to explain why men may be more likely than women to avoid intimacy, even within the context of marriage. As discussed earlier, women, as a result of their intuition and extensive experience, are better at relating emotionally than men. They are usually far more comfortable expressing and discussing their feelings, which is necessary to becoming emotionally intimate. In other words, when it comes to relationships, women have home-court advantage.

Men may feel as awkward sharing themselves emotionally as most women do playing pick-up basketball. Would you bet your most precious possession on your basketball abilities? People take risks when they feel comfortable about their ability to cover the risk. If a man is not confident in the arena of close relationships, risking vulnerability makes no sense to him. He concludes, "It is better to be safe than to be satisfied." Although a wife's fear of intimacy is not as obvious as her husband's, she may also struggle with taking the risk of vulnerability.

John and Shelly had been married for almost forty years. To most who knew them, they were a happy couple. They shared many interests including reading, tennis and biking. They had attended church together for as long as they had been married. They had shared in raising their three children, who now had families of their own. John was a successful lawyer who had always been deeply committed to his work. Shelly had put aside her professional career shortly after John finished law school. When the couple had children, Shelly spent the majority of her time caring for them. After the children were grown, she became actively involved in church and community projects. Only their closest friends knew that neither John nor Shelly would describe their relationship as close. Neither could remember the last time they had truly shared from their hearts. Their conversations were always courteous, but surface and factual.

John and Shelly decided to begin counseling after John was diagnosed with terminal cancer. Faced with death, neither knew how to share their vulnerable thoughts and feelings with the other. Shelly made a good argument that John always had kept matters rather superficial in the marriage due to his obsession with work. "He's never had time for me. I've always been near the bottom of his list of priorities," said Shelly. According to her, John was the classic case of a husband who neither wanted nor needed emotional intimacy in the marriage. Shelly shared how she had tried to draw close to John in the early years, but had given up after too many candlelight dinners were canceled while John burned the midnight oil at work.

Through the counseling process, both John and Shelly learned that they had spent many years of their marriage choosing safety over intimacy. Shelly had been deeply hurt by what she experienced as rejection early in their marriage. In response to that hurt, she began subtle ways of interacting with John that actually encouraged emotional distance between the two. For example, she frequently berated John for his obsession with work. She refused to listen to him talk about a big case he had won or a struggle with an associate. John began to feel that he could not share with Shelly his joy over success or his fear of failure. As a result, he withdrew even more into work. In the courtroom, he knew the rules and was respected by his colleagues. At home, he felt like a stumbling buffoon, incapable of saying the right thing to make his wife happy. The comforting choice always led him back to his office—leaving his lonely wife at home.

Although both were well-meaning, John and Shelly both contributed to their emotional distance. Both made the choice to remain safe rather than strive for greater intimacy in their relationship. It wasn't a decision that was made consciously. Rather, it had evolved after thousands of small choices over the years. Each day of their marriage presented the couple with opportunities to make little steps either toward each other or away from each other. When confronted with the crisis of John's illness, they realized that the foundation of their relationship had slowly eroded over the years.

Intimacy requires that both individuals meet each other at the deepest point of their need. Mutual insecurities and humanity are exposed without defense, so that the other may choose to either embrace the need or exploit the vulnerability. *Ultimately, for emotional intimacy to grow, each partner must be willing to meet the other's deepest needs and protect the other's greatest vulnerability.* This produces an environment of trust, allowing each other to feel safe to share more. However, when vulnerability is met with rejection and pain, both the husband and wife naturally move away from sharing and toward self-protection. They each develop their unique ways of living together, but stay emotionally safe . . . and distant. Like John and Shelly's marriage, all relationships build upon momentum. Every marriage is either moving toward greater intimacy or fleeing toward rigid self-protection.

The Keys to Safety in Intimacy

Let's face it. Relationships, especially close ones, can be very scary. All of us have experienced the pain of rejection or abandonment sometime throughout our lives. Those painful lessons stick with us and motivate us to avoid feeling vulnerable. Ironically, our deepest needs in marriage can only be met if we are willing to expose our greatest vulnerabilities.

Most women are aware of what they need emotionally from their husbands. It boils down to two words: value and safety. Picture a delicate, beautifully crafted vase. With its unique grooves in the crystal, there is only one like it in the world. To fulfill the purpose for which this vase was designed, its value must be appreciated and its delicacy must be protected. This precious, fragile vase is very similar to a married woman.

What a wife needs to emotionally "survive" in marriage is to be cherished by her husband. She is, therefore, vulnerable to his rejection. This rejection can take many forms, but always communicates the same thought: "I know you intimately, and you are at heart an unlovable person." What a devastating message! When a woman takes the risk of intimacy and allows another to know what is behind the masks she wears, she is open to either love or the ultimate rejection.

The need to feel greatly valued explains why women are so often wounded by their husbands' choice of activities. When he decides to go golfing with his buddies, his wife interprets this action as, "he values his friends more than he values me." If a man spends sixty-five hours a week at work, his wife concludes that his work is more important than their relationship. In the same way, spending $8,000 on a new motorcycle means he would rather spend his money on boy toys than on the love of his life.

"I'm just not important to you! You don't care about me!" How often do wives want to scream this to their husbands? Forgotten birthdays, hours in front of the television, lifeless conversation—these are some of the signals convincing a wife of how worthless she is in her husband's eyes.

The second emotional need for a woman in marriage is to feel secure. An argument can be made that in many ways, women are as strong as men. Both science and history have proven the incredible physical and emotional resources of a woman. However, men are naturally physically stronger than most women. Ideally, a man's strength is a great asset to his wife. He can protect her from physical dangers and accomplish tasks that she cannot.

Unfortunately, a man's booming voice, powerful muscles and stature can be used to intimidate rather than to protect. In order for intimacy to occur in marriage, a woman must be absolutely certain that her husband's strength will be used to protect rather than to harm.

A woman's need for security goes beyond the physical aspect. The position of submission naturally puts a wife in a vulnerable position. How can she trust the leadership of a man with whom she does not feel protected? Instead of trusting, she is likely to build a shell of defensiveness and hostility to protect herself. She becomes hard, bitter and critical to make sure that she is not hurt again. This defense naturally conceals her femininity and eliminates the possibility for a gentle and sensitive spirit. She has to be "tough" for the sake of her survival. She sacrifices her unique ability to meet the emotional needs of those around her.

Women who are neither valued nor protected in their marriages often describe feeling as if a part of them is dead. They may go through the motions of work, raising the children and even community involvement. However, they operate mechanically, without the passion and love that is their lifeblood. Afraid to trust, afraid to feel, afraid to really live.

Husbands can be afraid, too. Just like their wives, men have needs within marriage that must be met in order for intimacy to be possible.

It is very important for a husband to feel that he is a good leader and provider. He wants to be admired and respected for the way he cares for his wife and children. Yes, he wants to be a hero. The rejection that a man dreads is to be seen as incompetent or unable to live up to what is expected of him. His abilities to lead, provide and protect are central to his manhood. His wife's evaluation of him in these roles determines whether or not he is competent.

A man's insecurities and self-doubts are naked before his wife in the marriage relationship. He can no longer pretend to be the invincible knight that he was when dating her, or the unshakable genius in the workplace. He is sometimes afraid to take risks, and he is terrified at the thought of leading his family the wrong way. In the closeness of marriage, his wife knows his fears and instinctively is alerted to his feelings of inadequacy. She can capitalize on these vulnerabilities, or she can support him in spite of them.

My father shared a childhood story that is revealing of a man's need for support. He was about ten years old and desperately wanted to be liked by the other boys in his neighborhood. Through odd jobs and saving, he scrounged up enough money to buy a baseball glove. My dad was very excited to be a part of the local baseball team. During one of his first games, he dropped the pop fly that allowed the other team to win the game. All of the kids on his team harassed and rejected him.

As my dad relayed this story to me, it seemed as if he were reliving it. The pain of failing, of letting the team down, left a lasting impression.

Imagine this little boy. What a difference his parents could make by the way they responded to him. They could add to his humiliation and defeat by scorning him, teasing him or by even ignoring what he felt. On the other hand, they could encourage him greatly with a pat on the back, a trip to the ice cream store or a few words of unconditional love and support.

Is your husband a boy in a baseball game? The surroundings are different, but the fears are the same. What will you do with his vulnerability when he "drops the ball?"

Husbands are also vulnerable to their wives for the companionship that only they can provide. Certainly sexual companionship is a part of this. However, men need more from their wives than sex—men need their wives' input and influence.

Like women, men are capable of character flaws, times of particular vulnerability and harmful thoughts and motives. Without the input and accountability of an involved teammate, these chinks in his armor can lead to the devastation of the family.

Think of a man wrestling with the struggles of a mid-life crisis. He may begin to fantasize about being with other women and may even take steps toward experiencing this fantasy. However, if his wife is emotionally by his side, striving to understand his fears and encouraging him to pursue his dream of being a godly man, he is less likely to act out his destructive urges.

There are countless examples of ways a man can fall if he

lacks the companionship and accountability of a trusted partner.

Chris was a much stronger person than his wife, Cheryl, in many ways. His voice was loud and strong, his manner confident. Cheryl, as a shy and retiring personality, had no difficulty trusting Chris's leadership for their family. She sometimes listened to him explain his problems at work and heard him talk about someday wanting to own his own business. However, she shied away from giving him input, thinking that he was smarter and that she needed to trust his judgment. One day, Chris was fed up with the pressures of his job and impulsively quit. He returned home determined to begin his own business selling cellular telephones. To start his business, Chris took out a second mortgage on their home, cashed in his retirement fund and liquidated many of the family's assets. Cheryl was a little nervous, but decided that her role as a wife was to submit and respect Chris. Unfortunately, Chris's business failed within months. The couple was forced to declare bankruptcy.

Imagine what must happen between a couple like Chris and Cheryl. He feels like an absolute failure and has nowhere to turn. She deeply resents him and will have difficulty trusting any of his future decisions.

This dynamic is what often occurs when a wife understands her husband's need for respect, but not for companionship. Cheryl could have been a valuable partner to Chris by asking him about the risks he was taking. She could have helped him endure a stressful job situation while they planned together for a solution that would not lead to financial disaster. Husbands need their wives to be active partners in the areas of business decisions, finances, child rearing and relationships. Without this companionship, men become extremely vulnerable to their own blind spots, weaknesses and biases. This can lead to destructive consequences.

A healthy marriage is much like two puzzle pieces. It takes the protection of a man to bring forth the beauty of a woman. Likewise, it takes the sensitivity of a woman to bring out the valor of a man.

The Cycle of Intimacy

Within the context of intimacy, women need to be valued and protected, while men need to be respected and connected. In marriage, a wife is vulnerable to being seen as unlovable and a husband is vulnerable to being seen as incompetent. The primary message to husbands in the Bible can be summed up by "love your wife." The central message to wives is "respect your husband." God's unique instructions to husband and wife marvelously assures that both of their deepest needs are met and their greatest vulnerabilities protected. God's design for marriage intrinsically supports a cycle of growing intimacy.

When a husband loves his wife, he treats her with great sensitivity and care. He communicates to her that she is important to him and that he would sacrifice anything for her. He listens to her needs and concerns, and he makes decisions that benefit them both. His desire is to shelter her, please her and help her flourish as a godly woman. She learns that her role as wife is vitally important and fulfilling.

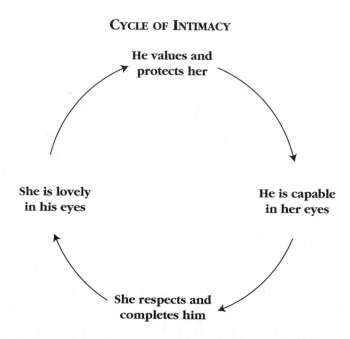

CYCLE OF INTIMACY

He values and protects her

He is capable in her eyes

She respects and completes him

She is lovely in his eyes

Any woman who feels cherished and protected by her husband cannot help but see him as her knight in shining armor. He is capable of providing for her emotional needs and becomes a hero in her eyes. God's command that she respect and yield to this man's leadership becomes easier to obey. After all, he is looking out for her interests. He is interested in her opinion and her feelings. She is confident that with her input, he will be a great leader for their family.

As she begins to treat her husband with admiration and respect, she becomes more and more valuable to him. More than anything, he wants her confidence and support. He wants her to trust him and believe in him. As she begins to do that, he thrives. He starts to see his wife as the most wonderful, supportive and beautiful woman in the world. She is so valuable to him that he does not know what he would do without her. God's command to love her becomes easier with each day because she is growing more lovable.

Doesn't this dynamic sound absolutely wonderful? Nothing could be more romantic and satisfying. After all, this is what every woman desperately hopes for when she approaches the wedding chapel. A glimpse of this intimacy is like a drug. Even if it vanishes in thin air shortly after it appears, it is worth going after.

Believe it or not, men yearn for this dynamic as much as women do. Their affairs with their coworkers are not just about sex. Often men get a taste of being admired, respected and listened to, and if it disappears in their marriage, they will seek it out elsewhere. The challenge is that few marriages can sustain this cycle of increased intimacy. It is rare that a man and woman choose to grow daily in their trust and more comfortable in their vulnerability. It is truly a miracle, and only by God's design does it occur.

We Are Not in Eden Any More

No matter how sensitive and well-meaning they may be, every husband and wife will fail under the spotlight of intimacy. Try as they might, it is impossible to always meet each other's needs and never tread on one another's vulnerability. Husbands and wives are, after all, only human. In the daily interchange of marriage there are hundreds of opportunities to either build trust or tear it down. In good marriages, most of those opportunities result in responding to needs and protecting each other from harm. However, every couple faces the inevitable betrayal of trust, whether intentional or not. It happens every day, in big ways and small.

As any mother of small children knows, caring for little ones can be a very tiring process. My personal experience is that a day of chasing toddlers, setting limits, nursing babies, changing diapers and cleaning up messes inevitably leads to exhaustion. Although I do not like cooking, I try to provide dinners that are healthy, cost-effective and pleasing to everyone. Every now and then, I make the extra effort of cooking something special that I think my husband, Mike, will enjoy. If I am really organized, I plan to have dinner on the table when he walks through the door. Imagining his delight when he sees his favorite dinner keeps me going. I cannot wait to feel appreciated and loved for my gesture. I know that it will help us on the cycle of intimacy.

You know the ending of this story before you read it because you have been there, too! Mike is running late. Dinner is cold and the kids are hungry. Mike comes through the door, frustrated at the traffic on his drive home. He looks at my beautiful dinner, gives me a kiss and says, "I'm sorry, Honey, but I grabbed an Arby's sandwich on my way home." Devastation! I feed the kids and stomp around all night. Never again will I sacrifice my time and energy trying to do something nice for him! So much for intimacy!

This is an example of the small breaches in trust and vul-nerability that inevitably occur in every marriage. Of course, a rejected dinner is much easier to recover from than rejected ideas or feelings. In reality, many women feel their husbands have rejected them in every way, through extramarital affairs or abusive interactions. However, the small hurts and breaches of trust are what ultimately lead to marital devastation for many.

Scott Stanley's research in *Fighting for Your Marriage* concluded that the greatest predictor of marital success and failure is how a couple deals with the little conflicts that they encounter every day. In the long run, what matters most is how the couple recovers intimacy when they get lost on the way to the party, when he says something that hurts her feelings or when she criticizes his financial decision. It is invariably the little things that bump a couple off the cycle of intimacy and onto a cycle of defensiveness. Guarding against additional hurt, each person seeks self-protection. Both become less concerned with meeting the other's needs. Instead, they succumb to the temptation to exploit the other's vulnerability because the exploiter becomes more powerful and safer than the victim.

The Cycle of Self-Protection

The cycle of self-protection is the exact opposite of God's design for intimacy in marriage. However, it is where many husbands and wives live. It is the wide and easy road that leads to the destruction of trust and love.

When a husband begins to see his wife as defective in some way, he naturally communicates this to her. Perhaps he makes comments about her weight, her intelligence or her cooking. He may unfavorably compare her to a friend's wife, who excels both at home and at work. His dissatisfaction may also be apparent in what he does not do. He may stop complimenting or encouraging her. He may drop hints that he would rather be with someone else. In essence, his actions communicate that he does not value her. Instead of using his

CYCLE OF SELF-PROTECTION

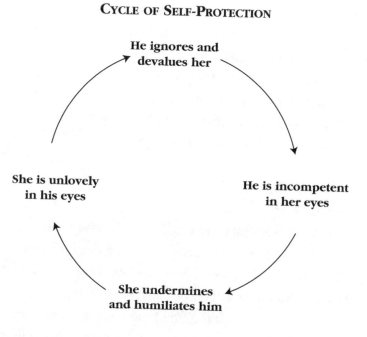

He ignores and
devalues her

She is unlovely
in his eyes

He is incompetent
in her eyes

She undermines
and humiliates him

strength to protect her physically and emotionally, he attacks her at her point of vulnerability. He may also use his leadership to get his own way, to her detriment.

The natural reaction of his wife is to view him as incapable of meeting her needs. In fact, this man is incompetent. She cannot trust his leadership. He'll lead her right into a pit of depression. To protect herself from his incompetence or insensitivity, she takes charge. She emasculates him through domination, manipulation or humiliation.

He may not even be aware of what his wife is doing, but he knows that he feels terrible about himself—especially when he is with her. Over time, he would rather be anywhere else. He cringes when he sees her friends, wondering what she has told them about him.

The strong, supportive woman he thought he married has turned into a nagging menace. She is a constant reminder of his failures, his weakness and his incompetence. He draws further and further away. Over time, the two are so emotionally distant that he could not even guess what his wife's real needs are. The cycle continues. His growing withdrawal continues to build on his failure in her eyes.

But He Started It!

From both scriptural references and observation, most people agree that men are designed to be the initiators in a relationship. Many women who find themselves in the cycle of self-protection blame their husbands for getting them there. Women often believe that their marriages are doomed because their husbands have proven to be incompetent at meeting the wives' needs to be cherished and protected. Perhaps if they had husbands who initiated the cycle of intimacy, their marriages would be headed in the right direction. After all, are women not designed to respond to their husbands' initiative and leadership?

The wonderful thing about a cycle is that it can be initiated at any point. Yes, the best-case scenario is for the man to create an atmosphere of intimacy with his initiative. However, women married to men who cannot or will not take this first step are not necessarily doomed to a lifetime of emotional hide and seek.

After fifteen years of marriage, Patti and Robert were definitely in an ingrained pattern of self-protection. Patti was ready to give up on the prospect of intimacy. "I have read the books and gone to the seminars, but nothing has made the difference for us," she lamented. "He just plays on his computer and works on his cars. Any time I try to initiate a conversation, all I get is one-word answers. At this point, I think we are happier when we are in separate rooms!"

Patti was taking the initiative to increase intimacy in their marriage. She was the one who came to counseling. She tried everything she knew to do to improve their marriage, without success. The main problem with Patti's attempt to draw her husband into intimacy was that she did not understand Robert's needs. She approached him the way she would like to be approached. Patti assumed that Robert needed to feel valued and loved in the way that she yearned to be appreciated. She did this by trying to ask about his day, telling him that she wanted to be closer to him and sharing her frustrations. Her attempts to draw Robert closer only left Patti feeling more neglected and isolated.

Through counseling, Patti learned how to intervene at her point of influence in the cycle of intimacy. She began to understand Robert's unique vulnerability as a husband. More than feeling loved, he needed to feel competent and respected as Patti's husband. Robert was experiencing great difficulty in his job. In fact, Patti's career had become more successful than his. Patti realized that many of her attempts to draw Robert into their relationship were actually threatening to him. By sharing her desire to be closer to him, she was telling Robert that he was an incapable husband. While he assumed that they had a good marriage, she complained about how unfulfilled she was. Instead of meeting his emotional needs, she had been unwittingly pouring salt in his wound.

Over time, Patti started to take small steps to encourage and empower Robert. She made a concerted effort to trust his leadership and to communicate her support. Instead of talking about how well things were going for her at work, she focused on Robert's success. She asked Robert his opinion about decisions she faced. Within a short period of time, Robert responded by drawing close to Patti.

Instead of wallowing in loneliness and frustration, Patti used her influence to change the cycle of her marriage. She set aside her needs temporarily in order to focus on her husband's feelings of isolation. She took the risk of vulnerability by initiating closeness in ways Robert would appreciate; she addressed her husband's deepest needs. It did not take long for Robert to respond. Because Patti was meeting his emotional needs, Robert was able to give his wife the closeness and love that she needed in their relationship.

Every marriage is in either the cycle of intimacy or the cycle of self-defensiveness. Momentum is either drawing husband and wife toward greater trust or repelling each further into their recesses of self-protection. It only takes one person to change that momentum and begin a new cycle. Just as one cutting remark can spoil the feeling of safety and intimacy, so can a small gesture of trust and vulnerability prepare the relationship for growth.

God has equipped a husband with the power to create an atmosphere that either facilitates vulnerability or encourages defensiveness. A loving, sensitive and capable man naturally sets the tone for emotional intimacy in the marriage. A man who uses his strength to violate or who clumsily bruises his wife's feelings at every step will soon be living with a woman who is emotionally isolated from him.

Women are very cognizant of the power that the men they love have over them. However, they often underestimate the influence that God has given them as women to affect the emotional and spiritual health of their intimate relationships. Although far more subtle than her husband's power, a wife has perhaps even greater impact on the emotional momentum in their relationship. Whether or not she realizes it, she has a great deal of influence over whether they are drawing closer to each other or further apart.

The wise woman builds her house, but with her own hands the foolish one tears hers down.

Proverbs 14:1, NIV

Questions for Discussion and Reflection

1. Why are intimacy and self-protection incompatible? (Read I John 4:18.)

2. Why are many men more hesitant when it comes to intimacy? Do you think a man's need for intimacy in marriage is different than his wife's? Why or why not?

3. What are your two greatest emotional needs as a wife? To what extent are these needs currently being met? How might your fear discourage you from seeking intimacy with your husband?

4. What are your husband's two greatest emotional needs in marriage? To what extent are you meeting these needs? How might his feelings of vulnerability discourage him from seeking intimacy with you?

5. Rate the amount of anger that has built up between you and your husband:

1	2	3	4	5	6	7	8	9	10
None		Mild		Moderate		Major		Absolute	

   What is the main source of your anger toward your husband? How does it interfere with your willingness to work on your marriage? Why is the anger so difficult to let go of?

6. Which way is the momentum in your marriage going—toward greater intimacy or toward self-protection?

7. What are some practical things that you can do to initiate a cycle of intimacy in the next week? (Read I Corinthians 13:1–8 for an explanation of perfect love).

6757058862

READER/CUSTOMER CARE SURVEY

We care about your opinions. Please take a moment to fill out this Reader Survey card and mail it back to us.
As a special "**thank you**" we'll send you exciting news about interesting books and a valuable **Gift Certificate**

Please PRINT using ALL CAPITALS

BA1

First Name [   ] Last Name [   ]

Address [   ]

City [   ] ST [   ] Zip [   ]

Phone # ([   ]) [   ] - [   ]   Fax # ([   ]) [   ] - [   ]

Email [   ]

(1) Gender:
O Female
O Male

(2) Age:
O 13-19   O 40-49
O 20-29   O 50-59
O 30-39   O 60+

(3) Your children's age(s):
Please fill in all that apply:
O 6 or Under   O 15-18
O 7-10   O 19+
O 11-14

(8) Marital Status:
O Married
O Single
O Divorced / Widowed

(9) Was this book:
O Purchased For Yourself?
O Received As a Gift?

(10) How many HCI books have you bought or read?
O 1   O 3
O 2   O 4+

(11) Did this book meet your expectations?
O Yes
O No

(12) How did you find out about this book? *Please fill in ONE.*
O Personal Recommendation
O Store Display
O TV/Radio Program
O Bestseller List
O Website
O Advertisement/Article or Book
O Catalog or Mailing
O Other _____

(13) What FIVE subject areas do you enjoy reading about most? *Rank only FIVE.*
Choose 1 for your favorite, 2 for second favorite, etc.

	1 2 3 4 5
Self Development	OOOOO
Parenting	OOOOO
Spirituality/Inspiration	OOOOO
Family and Relationships	OOOOO
Health and Nutrition	OOOOO
Recovery	OOOOO
Business/Professional	OOOOO
Entertainment	OOOOO
Sports	OOOOO
Teen Issues	OOOOO
Pets	OOOOO

FOLD HERE

BA1

9396058864

(25) Are you:
○ A Parent?
○ A Grandparent

(18) Where do you purchase most of your books?
Please fill in your top TWO choices only.
○ General Bookstore
○ Religious Bookstore
○ Warehouse / Price Club
○ Discount or Other Retail Store
○ Website
○ Book Club / Mail Order

(20) What type(s) of magazines do you SUBSCRIBE to?
Fill in up to FIVE categories.
○ Parenting
○ Sports
○ Fashion
○ Business / Professional
○ World News / Current Events
○ General Entertainment
○ Homemaking, Cooking, Crafts
○ Women's Issues
○ Other (please specify) _____

❧ *Six* ❧

My Prince
Turned Into a Frog!

Coup d'etat: a political word that can strike fear in leaders around the world. A *coup d'etat* occurs when a small group of individuals overthrows the government because they are unhappy with those who are currently in power. Although a *coup d'etat* may be an important step in removing a wicked or incompetent leader from power, it is inevitably a violent and painful process.

Fortunately, Western democracies have more peaceful ways of changing their government leadership. Although a political *coup d'etat* rarely happens in America, domestic revolutions occur daily. Many women decide that, for some reason, their husbands are unfit to be the leaders in their households.

Violently or subtly, they declare their own personal *coup
d'etat*, hoping to restore peace and order as the new leader of
the home. Life may feel a little safer with her in control.
However, female leadership in the home has never been God's
design in marriage. It makes the prospect of intimacy virtually
impossible.

Author Margo Kaufman once said, "The only thing worse
than a man you can't control is a man you can." There is nothing romantic or comforting about the thought of a woman controlling or dominating her husband. Regardless, many women
willfully do so.

Why Do Women Take Over?

There are some very logical reasons why wives often decide
to take matters of leadership into their own hands. Sometimes
it is because of her fear of trusting or her need to control.
Other times, it is because of true deficits in her husband's
ability to effectively lead.

Sue and Keith entered counseling as a last resort. Their
marriage had disintegrated over time and the two were on the
verge of separation. They had married at a very young age
without knowing much about each other. Keith had a history
of both physical and sexual abuse as a child. As the responsibilities of adult life became a reality, Keith found himself
overwhelmed. He was crippled by feelings of inadequacy.
Keith never felt up to the challenges of financially providing
for his family or of assuming a leadership role.

Over the course of ten years of marriage, Keith and Sue had

four children. The pressure mounted as Keith continued to shy away from what he knew would be certain failure. He bounced from job to job, at times going for months without work. In the absence of his leadership, Sue gradually assumed more responsibility. At the time they entered counseling, Keith had become much like another child for Sue to care for. He felt defeated and victimized. Sue had become physically and emotionally exhausted after years of assuming responsibility for herself, the children and her husband. She was angry that her needs as a wife were constantly neglected.

Sue is an example of a woman who had to assume responsibility and leadership in order to keep her family afloat. Keith was unwilling to do so, and incapable of protecting and providing for his family. There are many husbands like Keith who place their wives in this very position, most often due to the husband's physical ailments, mental illness or selfishness. However, some wives view their husbands as unable to lead for less dramatic reasons.

Caroline did not trust her husband's leadership. Paul was a competent but very unemotional person. He often said and did things that hurt Caroline's feelings. Caroline believed that his decisions were selfish and that he was incapable of considering her needs. Over time, Caroline learned to fend for herself. She trusted herself far more than she trusted Paul. She decided she, not he, would run the family.

Caroline methodically eroded Paul's power until she became the one making the majority of the decisions for their family. The transfer of leadership was so subtle that Paul did not even realize what had happened. He just knew that he and

Caroline had become "one of those couples" that he had promised himself that they would never become.

Caroline's *coup d'etat* was not violent nor dramatic, but it was effective. Although Paul had deficits in his leadership style, Caroline's fears played a large role in her decision to give up on God's design for their marriage.

When confronted in counseling about her *coup d'etat,* Caroline admitted to feeling paralyzed by her fear of Paul's weakness. "How do I know he will make the right decisions for our family? There are many times when I disagree with how he wants to invest our money, discipline our children or approach conflicts. I trust my way more than I trust his."

Caroline's fear of Paul's leadership represents what many women feel. It is extremely difficult to trust another person's way of approaching life. Each of us has learned to solve problems our own way. Over time, the success of our method has trained us to rely on our tried and true approach to quiet our anxiety and assure us that everything will be okay. "Others might do it another way, but my way works for me." In marriage, we are asked to merge our perspectives with those of our husband. Letting go of our own way can create both anxiety and fear.

When I am faced with a problem, I work hard to solve it. I worry and ruminate, convincing myself that I can come up with a solution. My husband has the opposite approach. He handles stress by withdrawing or doing something fun. The more relaxed he appears, the more anxious I feel. I start to worry for both of us. My experience tells me that my approach is the only one to take. It is very difficult for me to rely on Mike's approach. I trust my way, not his.

©2001 Julie Anderson.

Herein lies the challenge of the wife's role in marriage. How does she use her influence, yet resist the desire to take over when she feels vulnerable?

Most men marry before their thirtieth birthdays. As much potential for leadership as they may have, they are young and inexperienced when they take their vows. Every husband will, to some extent, fail in his role of leader, lover, provider and protector. Every woman will, at some point, experience the fear of trusting a husband who is capable of making drastic mistakes. Some of their fears are well founded. However, wives must be aware of how their fear influences how they use their power in marriage. In the case of violent, exploitative leadership, a *coup d'etat* may be necessary for survival. But in many cases, God can use the influence of a godly, wise woman to help her husband competently assume the role to which he is called.

The temptation to stage a domestic *coup d'etat* is, perhaps, one of the greatest that a wife will ever face. Trusting is incredibly difficult, especially when a wife intimately knows the weaknesses of her husband. She knows where he is vulnerable. God gave her that knowledge to support and bolster his leadership. Resisting the urge to exploit that weakness out of fear is only possible through ultimately trusting God.

When a woman, consciously or unconsciously, decides that she cannot trust the leadership of her husband, she begins to use her power and influence to weaken his confidence. Instead of protecting his vulnerabilities, she exploits them. She may assume leadership in a variety of ways, depending on both of their personalities and the culture around them. It is not only the aggressive, outspoken woman who may refuse to respect her husband. Some are far more subtle in their approach. In fact, many women have assumed leadership in their marriage without consciously knowing it. They are simply aware of the lack of intimacy and wonder why their husbands never meet their needs. They may never acknowledge their own part in refusing to meet his needs.

How Women Assume Leadership

There are three main strategies that wives tend to use to stage a *coup d'etat:* The Bulldozer, Kryptonite and The

Stealth Bomber. Although these strategies are drastically different in style and appearance, they all have similar results. No matter how a wife may assume the domestic leadership, she communicates to her husband that he is incompetent.

The Bulldozer

While growing up, one of my favorite television programs was *Little House on the Prairie.* In the middle of dramatic story lines, I could always count on a few laughs from the Oleson family: Nels, Harriet, Nellie and Willie. Everyone in Walnut Grove knew who wore the pants in that family. Harriet constantly bossed her husband around. Although Nels seemed like a really nice and capable man, Harriet used every weapon in her arsenal to defeat his leadership. The family dynamics of this dysfunctional group lightened up the program, but the state of their marriage represents a grave truth about many couples today.

You do not have to look far to find a couple who live like the Olesons. She makes all of the decisions and criticizes his leadership at every step. Perhaps he never wanted the responsibility of leading in the first place. In some marriages, the personalities naturally set up this dynamic. The husband may be passive and dependent by nature, while the wife has a take-charge style. Her personality may be so much stronger than his that male leadership would be like continually swimming upstream. If she is more educated or more intelligent, he may feel inferior to her and depend on her to make the decisions for the family. Perhaps he is afraid of failure, so he encourages his wife to take the initiative. For whatever reason, the couple becomes stuck in a pattern that is destructive to God's design for fulfillment and intimacy.

The Bulldozer wife is usually aware of what she is doing. In fact, everyone around the couple knows that she tends to dominate him. To the casual observer, she may appear to be a mothering type of wife who is always advising and scolding. "Don't put that cup on the table without a cup holder!" "How many times have I asked you not to watch that program with the kids around?" "You ordered a hot dog? You are supposed to watch your cholesterol!" Her motive is not to take charge, but to compensate for her husband's perceived limitations. It is the only way that she knows how to address the anxiety she feels about depending on a husband who fails in small or large ways.

A couple in this pattern has great difficulty making changes. They have adopted such a strong reversal in leadership for a reason. To some extent, they may both be comfortable with this compromise. However, it is not God's plan for a stable marriage. Their comfort rarely translates into intimacy. The wife can never relax in her husband's protection. She must bury her desire to be cherished as she assumes a masculine role. The husband is at heart humiliated by his weakness. His dreams to be respected fade daily as he settles for a role as a dependent. This couple is on very shaky ground.

Kryptonite

The superhero Superman had great powers, including flying, Samson-like strength and X-ray vision. However, he shriveled in weakness whenever his enemies exposed him to a special element called Kryptonite. Even if he could not see the Kryptonite, he was immediately weakened by its presence. Humiliation affects a man's confidence like Kryptonite affected Superman.

Jonathan Swift said, "Men are happy to be laughed at for their humor but not for their folly." Humiliation is the most devastating weapon to a man's confidence. Nothing kills the root of his manhood like being mocked.

The workplace can be a very humiliating atmosphere. For the sake of their own pride and power, some people humiliate their employees and coworkers. Marriage, ideally, should be a place of refuge from a world filled with criticism and rejection. Unfortunately, the home is sometimes the place where men experience the greatest humiliation.

Instead of building her husband's confidence, a wife can easily use the Kryptonite of words to destroy her husband's capacity to lead. The famous singer Barbra Streisand once said, "A bachelor is a man who is sometimes right." Another quote anonymously supports that thought: "A man may be a fool and not know it, but not if he's married." What a sad state of affairs when a man's integrity and confidence are at greatest risk in the marriage relationship!

Women can humiliate their husbands in a variety of ways. They may use direct statements like:

- "Right! A three-year-old could have figured that out."
- "I can't believe they actually promoted you!"
- "You can be so boring."
- "Maybe my mom was right about you all along!"

Humiliation can also come in more subtle ways that communicate the same message of failure and disrespect:

- "I have to work. We could never live on your paycheck."
- "You used to have such a muscular body."
- "The kids won't listen to you. I'll take care of it."
- "Maybe someday we will be able to afford a vacation."

One of the most common forms of humiliation is biting humor or teasing. It is very easy to laugh at another's expense. Even if no harm is intended, jokes can carry venomous poison. Jesting about appearance, sexuality, money, personality and past failures can be particularly damaging.

Teasing others may be an easy way to get a laugh, but the comic relief will come at great expense. A popular trend in television sitcoms is families taking verbal jabs at each other. *Roseanne, Married with Children, King of the Hill,* and *The Simpsons* are just a few examples. Husbands and wives compete to see who can humiliate the other more. Children sarcastically respond to their siblings and parents. Although less obvious, the destructive messages to American families are potentially as damaging to society as are those promoting graphic violence. Both adults and children are subtly influenced by this standard of family dynamics. (Michael Medved, an extraordinary columnist and movie critic, has authored two books, *Hollywood vs. America* and *Saving Childhood,* documenting how these trends in Hollywood have affected marriage and children in the United States.)

The most dangerous aspect of teasing is that it is difficult to defend against. For example, a wife teases her husband about his low pain tolerance. The whole family has the flu and he acts the most helpless of all. A few weeks later, she casually remarks with a laugh about what a hypochondriac he is; how he could never survive in the military. His face turns red and he defensively takes a cheap verbal shot at her. Their day continues with an obvious chill in the air.

Very few men will take the risk to say, "I don't like it when you tease me about that." If he were to say that, his wife may respond defensively, saying, "Well, it's true! You were a big baby when you were sick last week!" She continues to tease, releasing more Kryptonite and sapping her husband's strength.

Humiliation at home is destructive. However, it becomes lethal when done in the company of others. Women must be extremely careful about what they say about their husbands in public. I met with one couple in which the wife constantly told her friends about her husband's failures at work. She frequently complained about how he could not earn enough money to buy the things they wanted. This absolutely humiliated him in front of her friends. He could never trust her, not knowing what she might say about him at parties, on the phone and at church. Really sly wives can even use prayer requests as a way to humiliate their husbands publicly. "Please pray for Jim, because I think he might lose his job. He just doesn't know how to sell."

Being humiliated is certainly destructive to both a wife and a husband. A husband who constantly puts his wife down is not meeting her needs to be valued and protected as a woman. A wife who humiliates her husband is doing the exact opposite of showing him respect. She is telling him and the world that he is an incapable man who does not deserve respect. It will be impossible for the couple to experience intimacy in marriage in an atmosphere tainted by humiliation.

Humiliation can also be a backhanded way of expressing anger. Instead of telling her husband that he made her mad last night, a wife might retaliate by teasing him in front of others. In addition to damaging their relationship, teasing short-circuits the opportunity for conflict resolution. The couple may never address and resolve their anger towards each other.

The Stealth Bomber

Stealth bombers are one of the most effective weapons in a *coup d'etat,* not because of their force, but because they avoid detection. They silently slip past the radar and do massive damage to unsuspecting victims. As destructive as Bulldozers and Kryptonite may be to a man's confidence, nothing is more difficult to deal with than manipulation. Anyone can point out the dominating or humiliating wife, but the manipulative ones escape detection for a lifetime. Like a stealth bomber, manipulation exploits a husband's defenses without anyone ever knowing how it happened.

Not only does a husband rarely know when he is being manipulated, but often the wife does not even realize what she is doing. A woman can deceive herself, as well as everyone else around her, into believing that she is really acting in the best interest of her marriage. The Merriam-Webster dictionary defines the word *manipulate* as "to change by artful or unfair means as to serve one's purpose." Boy, are women good at this!

Men often are unaware of manipulation because it heavily relies on the subtleties at which women are more adept. Manipulation has the same goal as dominating and humiliating. A wife may resort to manipulation if she wants to challenge her husband's leadership without being obvious about what she is doing. If, for example, she is married to a strong man who will not let her dominate him, she may have to be sneaky about getting her way. Women also tend to manipulate if they fear what others may think if they were to take a more obvious route.

Once when I was speaking to a group of woman, one of them asked me, "What is the difference between manipulation and influence?" What a great question! Wives are called to use their influence to help their husbands—not to manipulate. The spirit of influence is to *help* him make a good decision based on giving him additional information. The motive of manipulating is to limit a person's choice by "stacking the deck" unfairly. Influence is overt and clear. However, manipulation can be subtle and deceptive.

Suppose I reason that for the sake of both health and appearance, my husband needs to lose some weight. I can influence my husband by sharing my concern with him. The choice remains his. He chooses not to go on a diet, so I become more desperate. I throw away any junk food that he brings into the house. I suggest that I might be more interested in his sexual advances if he lost weight. Now I am manipulating. I have used crafty measures to get him to do what I want.

Some wives are very skilled at manipulating. Each may have her own unique style, but a couple weapons of manipulation are quite common.

"I told you so."

These may be the four most despised words to a husband (except perhaps, "I have a headache"). Who wants to make a decision knowing that it will come back to haunt him if things go wrong? Life is filled with tough decisions and judgment calls. Sometimes the right choice is impossible to discern, but hindsight is 20/20.

No one likes to be wrong. However, failing is infinitely worse when someone rubs it in. I have a friend who used to call me right after one of my favorite sports teams would lose. Her reminder made my disappointment that much more painful.

So how does this relate to manipulation? "I told you so" does nothing to affect the outcome of the first decision, but it sends a strong message regarding how things should be handled in the future. If a husband knows that his wife will "let him have it" if his decision is wrong, he will naturally approach leadership with great apprehension. "I'll let her decide and face the chance of being wrong," he may reason. Or he may chose to do what his wife wants so that she can never blame him for making the wrong decision.

There are times in a marriage when saying or even implying "I told you so" seems absolutely necessary. A wife who lets her husband have that final say may feel absolutely vindicated when her instinct turned out to be right. Sometimes even a gloating glance is enough to communicate, "If only you would have listened to me!"

Whenever those four words scream to be aired, they are in reality totally unnecessary. A husband knows when his wife was right. To put it under his nose can result in only two things: him abdicating his leadership or becoming more desperate to prove that he is capable. Neither outcome builds the marriage.

When a wife is right, but resists the temptation to gloat in it, her encouragement goes a long way in building her husband's confidence. He feels less threatened and, therefore, more willing to consider her perspective in future decisions. By refusing to manipulate, she may give up an immediate opportunity to gain the upper hand, but she moves closer to becoming a truly influential wife.

Acting as if

This is a tricky form of manipulation, indeed. A wife may know her husband would not agree with something but proceed without letting him state that fact. This mirrors the old saying, "It's easier to ask forgiveness than to ask permission."

I have tried this tool before in our marriage, I regret to admit. As parents of two very young children, Mike and I try hard to limit our schedules and to avoid becoming overcommitted. We juggle our responsibilities at home, work and church to minimize the amount of time away from our sons. Mike also helps me with my tendency to say "yes" to every offer and opportunity. He knows that I will eventually stress out, burn out and freak out.

Every now and then, an opportunity arises for me to be involved in a ministry that I just cannot resist. I know that if I run it by Mike, he will remind me of how stretched I am already. He will tell me that saying "yes" to something else means saying "no" to the boys and to him.

Sometimes I commit myself without ever talking to Mike about it. I want to avoid his objections and even his input. Months later, the commitment shows up on the family calendar. By this time, it is too late for me to back out. "I thought I mentioned it to you," or, "I'm sorry. It just slipped my mind!" Pretty manipulative, huh?

"Acting as if" is a dirty trick. It is a backhanded way of getting what you want without appearing overbearing or dominant. Particularly when a decision involves both the husband and wife or affects the entire family, it is not fair to act under the assumption that he will agree in order to avoid a conflict. If you and your husband disagree about something, see it through. If need be, let him know what you are doing, even if he disagrees with it. However, using deception to get your way will erode trust and breed anger.

The role of the martyr

"Whatever you want dear. I only want to please you," Angela replies when her husband, Drew, asks where she wants to eat. He chooses a seafood restaurant. Angela browses through the menu with a pout on her face. "Anything wrong?" Drew asks. "No. Just looking over the menu," she replies.

When the food comes, Angela picks around her seafood pasta, barely eating anything. "Poor me," she thinks. "All I am is a servant. No one ever cares about what I need." Drew sees the pouty look on her face and becomes frustrated that he cannot make her happy. Angela did not like her dinner, but she earned a bargaining chip to be used at a later date.

Some wives have perfected the pout and the sigh. They are careful to keep their opinions subdued, but whenever things do not go their way, they expertly communicate, " I have spent my life serving you and you don't care about me." Ironically, they may even say, "Don't worry about me. My needs don't really matter. You go ahead and do what you want. I will be okay."

Women who play the martyr role do so because it yields great power. Guilt, guilt, guilt! They rarely state what they really want, but their husbands know when they are displeased. Eventually, he will bend over backward to keep her happy. He would rather give up his ideas and desires than be confronted with her histrionic misery when he makes the wrong decision. Even though a martyr plays the part of a helpless victim, she actually controls her husband in a subtle, yet powerful, manner.

Turn on the faucets

While driving to work one day, lost in my thoughts, I realized, too late, that I had just passed a speed trap. Sure enough, I turned the bend to find a police officer signaling me into a parking lot. I was only nineteen and this was my first ticket. Immediately I was filled with dread and fear. My mind started working. How could I avoid this ticket?

I felt a ray of hope as I noticed the officer was male. "No man can stand it when a woman cries," I thought. Because I was afraid and flustered, it was not difficult to produce a whimper and some real tears. Sure enough, the fatherly police officer was sympathetic to my terror. He let me off with a warning to watch my speed and a reassuring smile.

For some men, tears are a powerful influence. A crying wife often makes a man feel helpless and like a bully. His instincts may be to rally by her side and do whatever it takes to soothe her pain. A manipulative woman can easily use this to her advantage. A fitting parallel is a man with a screaming child who desperately gives the child anything to stop the crying.

Crying can be a very appropriate method of expressing sadness and frustration. Sometimes, it is necessary to communicate desperation or simply to release pent-up emotion. Often, tears are an important means of getting a husband's attention. However, when they are intentionally conjured to short-circuit a conflict or to reach a desired outcome, tears are manipulative.

Retaliation

Laurie hates the television. Her husband, Greg, likes to relax by sitting in his recliner and channel surfing. Whenever Greg turns on the television, Laurie huffs around the house. "He knows I can't stand it when he watches TV. What a colossal waste of time. Why doesn't he help me with the kids?" she fumes under her breath.

When he finally shuts off the television, Greg approaches Laurie to give her a hug. Her body stiffens. Greg goes to the den to pays some bills. Meanwhile, Laurie makes dinner for herself and the kids and leaves a frozen dinner on the counter for Greg. Greg gets the picture. He is well aware of the consequences of watching television!

A spending spree, a chilly mood, withholding sex or "forgetting" something important to him are all ways that a wife can "punish" her husband. Whether he made a bad decision, was insensitive or forgot their anniversary, he will somehow suffer for his mistake. When it comes time to make decisions, he is well aware of what will happen if he blunders. Therefore, his wife has power and control over what he decides and how he acts. He is not acting out of love for her, but out of fear of what she might do if she does not get what she wants.

Manipulation sounds cruel. However, most women who manipulate do not do it because they are mean-spirited or because they want to overtly control their husbands. Many of them truly believe they are doing what is best for their marriage.

Although the manipulative wife is not obviously destructive, the damage she inflicts on her husband can be just as ravaging as the more blatant qualities of domination and humiliation. She often treats him like a child, making decisions for him behind his back. She may choose his friends by conveniently keeping him busy at certain times. She may discourage his hobbies by ensuring that he never has the time or money. She may control the money by spending without regard to the budget they agreed upon. Her challenge to his leadership is passive but very effective. In fact, he likely will not even know he has been challenged. He just instinctively senses that he cannot trust her, that she is not in his corner.

The danger of the Stealth Bomber is that she can convince herself that she is submissive and respectful of her husband. As she deceives him and all those around her, she often deceives herself. She justifies her meddling as being for his own good. "He needs me to do this," she rationalizes. But what she is really communicating is that he is incapable of making good decisions without her interference. Instead of helping him, she forces him into a decision. Even if the immediate outcome in favorable, the process is deceptive.

Ultimately, it ends in self-protection rather than the trust required for intimacy to occur.

So What Can I Do?

The fear of trusting a fallible man to lead is genuine. Some women are married to men whose abilities to lead are severely flawed. When a man's leadership is clearly ungodly or destructive, she may have no other choice but to assume leadership. Husbands can potentially be both abusive and destructive. Certainly it is not right for a wife to support or to endure this leadership. Other men simply will not lead. There are times, as discussed in chapter four, when a godly woman must step into the leadership role to preserve the family from disaster. However, this should always be the exception rather than the rule.

Many women challenge their husband's leadership for far less justified reasons. The bottom line is that they want to be in control. These wives do not trust their husbands to be competent leaders; or they simply want to have things their own way.

Every wife will experience hurt, failure and disappointment. This presents her with a decision. Will she use her God-given power to help her husband grow into effective and godly leadership? Or will she stage a *coup d'etat,* afraid to trust God's design and the potential for growth in both of them? If she chooses the latter, she has eliminated the possibility of developing an intimate relationship with her husband. Both she and her husband will ultimately be unfulfilled because their deepest needs and desires are disregarded.

Through trusting a fallen man in the leadership of her home, a woman is really called to trust the Lord for His plan for the family. Scripture clearly teaches that God has called the husband to be the head of the household and the wife to respect and support his leadership. By refusing to follow God's plan, the *coup d'etat* is not only against her husband, but also against God's plan. What we should really be asking is not, "Can I trust my husband?" but "Can I trust my God and His plan for our family?"

Ultimately, it is not a prince on a white horse who will rescue a woman from her pain, depression and anxiety. It is a loving God who is the Savior. He knows the needs that He has created within each woman. Only He holds the key to meeting her deepest needs for intimacy, security and worth. He may choose to meet many of those needs through her husband. The Lord will meet the needs of those who seek Him. He will reward the righteousness of a woman who depends upon Him.

The wise woman builds her house, but with her own hands the foolish one tears hers down.

Proverbs 14:1, NIV

Questions for Discussion and Reflection

1. What is a domestic *coup d'etat?* Why would a wife want to take over the leadership of her family? Is there ever a good reason to do so?

2. When a wife becomes the leader of a family, what are the consequences to the husband? The wife? The children?

3. Have you ever been tempted to stage a *coup d'etat* in your marriage? If so, why? Which of your fears are justified and which are the result of your desire to have things your own way?

4. What style do you use to challenge your husband's leadership: Bulldozer, Kryptonite, or Stealth Bomber? Think of some specific examples of your attempts.

5. Read Psalm 46, 62:5–10, 118:8–9 and Matthew 6:25–34. How can you focus on trusting God when your trust in your husband subsides? How can you depend on God's leadership when you feel anxious?

6. What are three specific and practical things you can do to resist the urge to challenge your husband's leadership in your marriage?

Seven

Opposites
Fatally Attract

*O*pposites. Can't live with them; can't live without them! In a room filled with people, opposites magnetically attract each other. The talker finds the listener. The clown finds the stoic. The strong finds the weak.

Men and women often talk about meeting their soul mate, the one who will fill the void in their life and "complete" them. Their soul mate will possess every quality that they lack. Although the concept of a "completer" is certainly attractive, it does not always lead to a fulfilled, harmonious life. In fact, comedies are rife with examples of opposites trying to work around each other. Laverne and Shirley, Laurel and Hardy are two that come to mind. The funniest and probably the most lifelike example is from Neil Simon's *The Odd Couple*. Although they could not live without each other, Felix and Oscar drove each other nuts. The humor from *The Odd Couple* is so popular because many people experience the frustration of sharing their life with someone who is their opposite.

In many ways, my husband and I are a story of opposites attracting. As a twenty-year-old college student, I was as uptight as they come. I spent 95 percent of my college career either in the library or practicing tennis. Dating and recreation were occasional activities I enjoyed only when all of my work was done. Serious to a fault, I often walked down the sidewalk deep in thought, oblivious to those around me. Everything had to be accomplished and planned in my mind. I lived a sheltered and controlled life with no room for spontaneity or faith.

Then I met Mike, my knight in shining armor. He certainly had a serious side to him, but he was fun! He loved having a good time and making spur-of-the-moment decisions. He was so full of energy, life and faith. He had no idea what was in store for him in the years to come and trusted God totally for his leading and provisions.

We shared common goals and passions, but our personalities and experiences could not have been more different. While I played tennis, Mike served in the Marines. While I studied daily, he crammed for exams the night before. Mike and I were instantly attracted to each other. This made for an exciting courtship. I remember being on dates, with Mike usually goofing around. Out of the blue, I would ask questions like, "What are our goals in this relationship?" "Have you read any books lately?" "If we got married, what kind of schools would you want to send our kids to?" One time, Mike was playfully kissing my face and I protested, "Stop! Those kisses don't mean anything!"

We could both tell hundreds of humorous anecdotes of us trying to sort through our differences. I never thought we would end up married. However, as much as our dissimilarities caused tension, they also created a wonderful chemistry. I loved the spontaneity that Mike introduced to my life. We would be walking down the beach, and he would pick me up and run me into the water, clothes, shoes and all. He would surprise me at work with mystery dates. He challenged me to depend on God, rather than trying to control Him. He felt compassion for people in ways that I never had. I knew that this man could challenge me in ways that I needed to stretch. He helped me think outside of my rigid box.

Marrying someone who is very different provides a wonderful opportunity for balance. However, those same differences can result in stagnation and hostility virtually overnight.

Balance or Polarization?

Robin Williams and Sally Field co-starred in the humorous film, *Mrs. Doubtfire.* In the beginning of the movie, their characters are married with three children. Williams plays a loving father who is very much like a child himself. He indulges his children with junk food, loud music and constant entertainment. His wife is his polar opposite. She is sensible, responsible and boring.

One of the first scenes is the two of them preparing for their thirteen-year-old's birthday party. Mom picks up a cake and heads home to the quiet party she has planned for her son. She arrives to blaring music, kids (and dad) jumping on the furniture, and farm animals roaming around the house. In tears, she explains to her husband that she is tired of always being the "heavy." He has fun with the kids and she is the one who always has to say "no" and think responsibly. Her birthday cake could never compete with Dad's animals, music and chaos. The differences which had initially attracted them eventually drove them permanently apart.

Why do some couples draw closer through their differences while others learn to despise each other? In many marriages, like the one shown in *Mrs. Doubtfire,* one person is very responsible while the other tends to shirk and ignore responsibility. For argument's sake, we will assume the wife, Laura, is responsible while the husband, Joe, is not.

When these two marry in their twenties, they each have definite attitudes and tendencies toward responsibility. As they go through the newlywed process of dividing up roles and jobs, their differences become apparent. Laura may naturally assume more responsibility because she wants things done her way. Her husband certainly is not going to complain for getting less work. Perhaps Joe's only household jobs include paying the bills, taking out the garbage, mowing the grass and caring for the cars.

In the course of their first year of marriage, Joe forgets to pay some bills on time. His responsible wife answers the phone when the electric company calls threatening to shut off their power. She freaks out. Laura has never been delinquent. This will destroy her credit record! She frantically calls Joe at work. "The electric company called. Did you know we are two months late paying the bill?" He promises to take care of it soon.

After several such experiences of Joe forgetting and her nagging, Laura cannot stand the stress anymore. She decides that they would be better off if she paid the bills. Joe now has one less job. Several months later, Laura looks out the window and notices that the grass has not been mowed for three weeks. Irritated, she mentions something to her darling Joe. Another three days go by, and their lawn starts to look like a rain forest. She finally gets so angry that she mows it herself. Another job has now become hers.

This cycle goes on and on. Systematically, Laura assumes more and more of Joe's responsibilities. Down the road, she may spend more time at work to make up for Joe's lack of income. As his responsibilities diminish, Joe slips further into the mode of carelessness.

Joe and Laura were initially drawn to each other based upon their differences. "He is such a good balance for me," she said when they met. The original goal of this couple was to help each other to become more complete. However, the opposite has occurred. She became more responsible while he became less. Herein lies the danger of opposites.

Instead of a husband and wife helping each other grow in their weaknesses, they often stagnate in their limitations. Laura's behavior was driven by the fear of losing control. She could not stand the long grass, the unpaid bills or the uncertainty of Joe's job. Joe's refusal to take responsibility made her fears even greater. Instead of Joe helping her learn to relax, she became more anxious and compulsive.

Joe's weaknesses are his laziness and procrastination. Perhaps his parents always took care of things for him, never holding him accountable for his responsibilities. Laura repeated this pattern. By paying the bills and mowing the grass she communicated this: "If you are lazy long enough, I'll reward you by relieving you of any responsibility. I can't trust you enough to do the job right anyway!"

Laura is in her glory doing everything the right way and Joe is happy as a couch potato. What a perfect ending for the fairy tale, right? Not quite. Although Joe and Laura might feel comfortable in this arrangement, they can never feel happy or fulfilled. As a matter of fact, they probably are quite angry at each other. Laura resents the fact that she has to manage everything. She can never relax or trust Joe to take care of her. Joe resents Laura for not believing in him. He does not like the lump of lard that he has become and probably faults her for nagging him into idleness.

The Dance of Destruction

Differences in any area of personality can potentially create either growth or destruction in a marriage. Some common differences can include the morning person and the night person, the talker and the listener, the introvert and the extrovert, the spender and the saver. There are two aspects of personality that seem to present the greatest threat to intimacy when opposites marry: *Passive/Dominant* and *Selfish/Selfless.*

Passive/Dominant

These two are destined to find each other. Passive people fear making decisions for themselves. They lack confidence, direction and strength. They have survived by finding people to lead them and make decisions for them: parents, siblings, pastors, friends, counselors—anyone who can rescue them from ambiguity and insecurity.

Passive people are searching the world for a counterpart—a dominator. Dominant people love making decisions for themselves and for others. They must be in control and they always know the right thing to do. They are people of action. They are immediately drawn to people who admire and follow their leadership. They are comfortable only when people depend on them and support their dominance.

Although the world needs both leaders and followers, neither the passive nor the dominant person is likely to facilitate intimacy. They both relate based on their fears. Passive people fear being strong and dominant people fear being weak. They may seem to meet the other's needs. However, they are relating in ways that keeps both of them safely away from their respective fears. Neither will ever grow as long as he or she has the other.

Selfish/Selfless

Few would argue that selfishness is an intimacy killer. Selfish people live only for themselves. They think only of their own needs, goals and desires. They may be very good at masking their motives, but even their altruistic acts are driven by what they want to accomplish or achieve. There is no room for caring for others. If time allows they may perform a token considerate act, but only if it eventually benefits them. They seldom seek the input or best interest of their spouse. From where they will eat dinner to where they will live, their goal is to please themselves.

Selflessness is a little more tricky. Looking at these two styles, most people would immediately praise the selfless one. In fact, there are many scripture references that appear to encourage followers of Christ to become selfless in their relationships. Many present Christ as the example of ultimate selflessness.

There is a subtle, but important, difference between someone who is willing to serve and someone who is selfless. When people are selfless, they essentially deny their own needs, existence and influence. They try to melt into the scenery and make their own needs invisible. They live to adjust to the needs and demands of others.

The only aspect in which Christ was selfless was in relationship to God. He only denied his needs and desires in accordance to God's will and plan. However, he was not selfless with others. He approached people with great strength and determination. They did not change him, he changed them. Yes, he focused on meeting their needs *as his obedience to God led him!* There were many times when he did not give people what they wanted. In fact, he never indulged the selfishness of the Pharisees.

Selfless people serve out of weakness and fear rather than out of love and conviction. They avoid confrontation and are afraid of articulating their own needs. They fear rejection, and they serve to keep those around them in their favor. *A selfless person perfectly compliments a selfish person and enables him or her to ignore the needs of others.* A selfish husband will never learn to think about his wife if she denies her own needs. She must entrust her needs to him for intimacy to occur.

Being a servant to others does not require the absolute denial of your own physical, emotional and spiritual needs. Philippians 2:4 (NIV) says, "Each of you should look not only to your own interests, but also to the interests of others." Every person has needs that cannot consistently be ignored.

I recently noticed an illustration of this in my life. The other day, I came home from the grocery store with my two young children. It was 1:00 P.M. and we were all hungry. Michael, my three-year-old, had to use the bathroom, and Andrew had a stinky diaper. I had to go to the bathroom, too. So, what was I to do first? We all needed to eat and we all needed bathroom time. As a mom, I served my kids first. I took Michael to the bathroom and changed Andrew's diaper. Then it was my turn. After that was done, I fed the kids and then made myself something to eat. My love, commitment and care for my kids means that I meet their needs before meeting my own.

However, there is a time when I must take care of what I need. Imagine if I rationalized, "The kids need me to play with them now. It would be selfish for me to take the time to use the bathroom or eat lunch." Eventually, this selflessness would incapacitate me as a mother. Such an attitude would also create demanding, selfish children. They would get what they want NOW, regardless of the needs of others. Sometimes they need to wait for me to get off the phone before they ask me something. Sometimes they need to wait for me to finish eating before I play with them. Their needs are a priority, but not my *only* priority.

I know women who have divorced their husbands and abandoned their children claiming, "I need to find myself" or, "I want to focus on me for once." *This* is selfishness! Christians are called to be servants and to keep the needs of others high on their list of priorities. However, they are called to serve out of the strength of a commitment to God and to others. Their service should enrich and strengthen the lives of others, not enable insensitivity and selfishness.

A Deadly Combination

Most destructive relationships fall into a pattern that combines the styles of relating described. What results are the following dynamics:

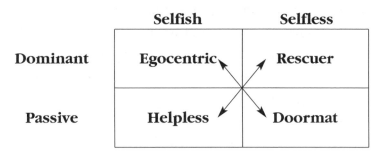

DESTRUCTIVE COMBINATIONS

	Selfish	Selfless
Dominant	Egocentric	Rescuer
Passive	Helpless	Doormat

Egocentric Meets Doormat

Egocentrics are dominant people who are solely focused on their own needs. They forcefully structure the dynamics of the family and their relationships to gratify themselves. Their dominance may come in the form of blatant bossiness or subtle manipulation.

An egocentric husband may hide under the facade of "male leadership." He makes all of the family decisions himself without even thinking about the impact on his family. He quickly becomes a dictator who has alienated himself from the ones whose love he desperately needs.

Wives can be egocentric, too. Such a wife is always in control, either overtly or subtly. She uses influence to tailor the marriage around her needs. She is so absorbed with what she wants from her husband that she is virtually unaware of what her husband needs from her.

Egocentrics develop this style based on their need for control. They believe that no one will ever look out for them so they must live for themselves. Their greatest fear is to be out of control of their own destiny. Trusting others (or even God) is not an option.

Sometimes they develop this belief based on a background of exploitation. Their past experiences have impressed upon them that they cannot trust others to meet their needs or look out for their best interests. Egocentrics also can emerge from childhoods in which their every need has been indulged. This can be particularly true of only children who were "worshipped" by the adults around them. They naturally assume that the world revolves around their own needs and desires. They see themselves as deserving of special attention and recognition and have great difficulty considering the needs of others.

Egocentrics think that a Doormat is the perfect partner for them. Doormats are both passive and selfless. Their needs never count. In fact, their needs seem to be nonexistent. Doormats naturally melt into their surroundings. They are easily controlled, ignored and exploited.

Movies and sitcoms from the fifties and sixties often present women as Doormats. Their husbands rule the home, while they seem happy expressing no thoughts and no opinions. Their needs are virtually invisible. The meager influence of these women goes to supporting the absolute power of their husbands.

A Doormat husband often works diligently every day of his life. Every week, he faithfully hands over his paycheck to his wife. He may even symbolically retain the role of leader in his house. However, all who live there understand that his power is token and he is a figurehead. He lives to serve and support his overpowering wife. He gives his strength and position to her.

Doormats are afraid of being noticed and harmed. They do everything in their power to avoid conflict. This is survival technique for them. As obnoxious as their Egocentric spouse may be to others, this is what is comfortable for a Doormat: someone who allows them to be both passive and invisible.

Rescuer Meets Helpless

Rescuers are dominant people who want to meet everyone else's needs. They use their influence and power to mold their relationships around the weaknesses of others. They often find themselves behaving more like a parent than a spouse. Rescuers often communicate, "I know what is best for you, dear. I will take care of you." They overtly and covertly makes decisions to accommodate and deliver those they love.

Although she may want to help others, a rescuer wife must ask herself why she is so invested in saving her husband. The answer often relates to her own need for security. A rescuer often believes that she is important only because others need her. If her husband needs her, then she does not have to fear his rejection. Although she may appear to be selfless, the rescuer is really acting based on her own fears and insecurities. A rescuing husband may like having a weak and needy wife. Maybe it is this that allows him to feel like the knight in shining armor. However, the role of savior is a heavy burden to carry. The rescuer will never allow himself to become truly vulnerable to his wife. He must always appear able and strong enough to carry her. In becoming her savior, he has eliminated the chance of becoming her friend, lover and teammate.

Rescuing spouses can unwittingly create havoc in their marriages. At an unconscious level, their goal may be to keep their partner stuck. If a rescuer's husband no longer needs her, then she is at risk for rejection. However, if he remains helpless, he will always be dependent upon her.

Somewhere down the road, someone will inevitably set the Rescuer up with a Helpless. Helpless husbands or wives simply cannot take care of themselves. Their limitations may be physical, spiritual or emotional. The bottom line is that they needs others to survive. Helpless spouses are passive and absorbed with the task of getting their own needs met. Since they cannot meet them, they must elicit the help of others.

Helpless wives usually have developed a tried and true strategy of attracting the compassion and resources of others. Sometimes they are attractive, warm and friendly. They may present as lost and helpless puppy dogs. Often their histories are tragic, naturally evoking the helper in their companions.

At times in their lives they have been helpless. However, they have never ventured out of the identity of a victim. Helpless wives live with the daily fear that they will be abandoned, left to their own feeble resources. They invest much of their energy into attracting those who are likely to care for them.

A helpless husband usually has a mother who did a little too much mothering. There is almost always a great mother-in-law story when it comes to such a man! Often his mom and his wife wage warfare over who is going to take care of poor Helpless. He lets them fight it out, resting assured that at least one of them will be there to provide direction and support. Unfortunately, the helpless husband never grows up. His wife, one day, wins the war with his mother. Not soon after, she *becomes* his mother.

Helpless is a natural fit with the Rescuer. Their needs are wonderfully complementary. Rescuers need someone to make them feel important and their Helpless partners need someone to provide continual direction and care. A match made in heaven! The only problem is that neither of them grows. In fact, they become more entrenched in their fears and their insecurities.

Opposites are so deadly because they naturally compensate for each other's weaknesses. Pairing an 80-pound anorexic and a 350-pound overeater will not help either of them. The anorexic will gladly hand her food over to her hungry companion. Their collective weights will never balance each other out. They will only reinforce the other's sickness.

Finding a New Dance

During the first few years of marriage, every couple irons out their "dance." They create a unique way of interacting that seems to create safety for both the husband and the wife. For example, the dominator makes the decisions and the passive partner politely obeys. Of course, they never sit down and decide, "You be the egocentric dictator and I will be the weak punching bag." It just happens. Their dance soon becomes entrenched in all areas of their marriage.

After years of marriage, literally thousands of experiences reinforce their dance. Very few couples endure the conflict and change that growth requires. They stick to their predetermined role. They dance very well. Their dance is as predictable as a scene from *The Odd Couple.* Anyone around them knows exactly how they will make decisions and what will happen when they fight. For example: he yells, she gives the silent treatment and he finally gives in to what she wants. Even they know the outcome, but they are forced to go through the petty scripts of yelling, arguing and pouting. It is the way they have always done it.

I have some friends who took a dance lesson together. The problem is that they only took one lesson. They know only one dance. Wherever they go, whatever the music, they do their one dance together. The dance is memorized and their movements are quite rigid. Their dance is impressive when the right music is playing, but it is hilarious when the tune changes. Fox-trotting to reggae is quite a scene! As much as they rehearse their dance, they are limited to a very specific type of music. When the band changes its tune, they either make fools of themselves or they must stop dancing.

Intimate marriages always have the rare trait of flexibility. There are times when both husband and wife will be active in making decisions. Sometimes his needs will be paramount and sometimes hers. They both know how to lead and follow. They both know how to meet the needs of others and articulate their own. Their dance is fluid. They are so intimate that they instinctively react to the subtle changes of the music, the rhythm and their partner. They seem to be like one body, perfectly complementing and leading the other toward strength and beauty. Their flexibility and perfect knowledge of each other allows them to dance adequately to any music. They are unafraid of learning a new move, knowing that even when they stumble, they will pick each other up.

After five, ten, twenty years of marriage, learning a new dance can seem like a daunting task. A woman who appeared to be in her seventies approached me after I had spoken on this topic. She explained that she and her husband had been stuck in the same dance for fifty years. She identified herself as an Egocentric married to a Doormat. "Is there any hope of us changing after all of these years?" she asked.

What a great attitude! There is always hope of change, even after fifty years of marriage. However, change is never easy—particularly changing something that has been reinforced for many years.

Lesson One: Accept That Your Dance Is Outdated

Film director William Rostler said, "You won't find a solution by saying there is no problem." This is often the hardest part of changing. Doing things the way they have always been done feels comfortable. Why change it if it seems to be working?

The real question is, is it really working? Husbands and wives are often *comfortable strangers* rather than *courageous intimates*. Chances are, if you could identify you and your husband in "the dance of destruction," you need some dancing lessons.

Lesson Two: It Takes Two to Tango

As frustrating as your husband may be, you most likely play some part in his irritating style. A rigid relationship pattern is only possible if there is a complementary pattern to support it. Sometimes a wife's role in the dance may not be obvious. I met with a woman whose husband was very irresponsible. He could not hold down a job for more than a few months and never lifted a finger around the house. Everyone around her felt sorry for her, but their sympathy did not make her marriage any better. Through counseling, she began to realize that she had gradually taken up the slack for her husband's irresponsibility. In the midst of trying to keep her family afloat, she was helping her husband sink the ship. She said, astounded, "I never realized I had a part in this!" She actually felt hopeful. Her part of the dance meant that she had the influence to change the dance. Her husband could not continue his destructive dance without her.

Lesson Three: Try the Mashed Potato
When He Does the Fox-Trot

Stop dancing to the same old music. Let's say that you are a rescuer who rescues your helpless husband. You make all of his decisions from what he has for lunch to what he wears to work. Although you like having control and influence, it drives you crazy that your husband seems so spineless. You want to say to him, "Make a decision for once in your life!"

Stop playing your role! If you do not pick out his suit, he has to. If you do not mow the lawn, he will have to deal with it. This is a very challenging task. You are not only fighting your own urge to rescue your husband, you are fighting his urge to be rescued. This is the hardest part about learning a new dance. The fox-trot is tempting. It is the way you have always danced. He will try to pull you into it again. The lawn may be five feet tall and drive you nuts before he finally gets around to it. But remember, intimacy and growth are more important than comfort. Former Secretary of State John Foster Dulles said, "The measure of success is not whether you have a tough problem to deal with, but whether it is the same problem you had last year."

Lesson Four: Remember to Stretch

Changing the dance means using muscles that you have never used. If you are a control freak, you have to learn how to trust and be quiet. If you are comfortable being dependent, you have to mature into making good decisions for yourself. If selfishness is your defect, seek God's help in caring for others. What seems unnatural will probably never be easy.

Part of changing is realizing why you are stuck. What fear keeps you in your rigid manner of relating to others? Losing control? Being dominated or harmed? Abandonment? These fears may be the essence of who you are and may seem too painful to address. Stretch those muscles with the support of a pastor, counselor or friend. Seek encouragement through the Bible and prayer. Author Richard Lewis once said, "If we don't change directions, we will arrive at where we are going."

Lesson Five: Listen to the Band

The music changes constantly in marriage. Most people marry in early adulthood. Think about all of the maturation the husband and wife will go through during their lifetimes. The two will deal with thousands of circumstances. These might include having children or infertility, job changes, layoffs, cancer, debt, family problems, church splits, impotence, depression, panic attacks, death of loved ones, and many others that could not possibly be predicted. Over the course of the years, the husband and wife must maintain their passions, beliefs and commitment. However, they must be flexible to the demands of the circumstances.

If a husband is always the person who makes the decisions, what happens when he goes through a period of depression? His wife must be able to carry his burden for a time. What if she develops cancer? Her husband will become responsible for taking care of the children in a new way. Successful marriages result from uncompromising commitment that is beautifully expressed whether the tune is a gleeful march or a solemn requiem.

Dear friends of ours, Pam and Steve, serve as role models of "great dancers" for Mike and me. Throughout the time we have known them, we have seen them respond to both good times and bad. There are many ways in which Pam and Steve are different from each other. For example, Steve is outspoken, while Pam loves to make others feel comfortable. Steve is a strict parent, while Pam is very nurturing. These two have used their differences to create a wonderful environment. Over the years, they have challenged each other to grow, rather than simply compensating for their respective limitations. As their circumstances have changed, they have adjusted to each other's needs. Every year that we have known them, their marriage continues to grow stronger rather than stagnating in complacency.

Differences between a husband and wife can result in a beautiful balance. Proverbs 27:17 (NIV) states, "As iron sharpens iron, so one man sharpens another." But sharpening iron means that sparks will fly. The growth that results from intimacy is not the easy road. It occurs when husband and wife courageously follow the beat of the Lord of the dance.

> *The wise woman builds her house, but with her own hands the foolish one tears hers down.*
>
> **Proverbs 14:1, NIV**

Questions for Reflection and Discussion

1. When a husband and wife are opposites, what causes them to either become balanced or polarized by their differences?

2. In what way are you and your husband opposites? How have these differences between you played out in your marriage?

3. Plot yourself and your husband on the following graph.

DESTRUCTIVE COMBINATIONS

	Selfish	Selfless
Dominant	Egocentric	Rescuer
Passive	Helpless	Doormat

Now plot where you would like for you and him to be. What fears may be keeping you and him from interacting differently?

4. In what ways has your marriage "dance" become inflexible or rigid? Why may it be difficult to try something new?

5. What are some practical steps you can take to break out of the same old patterns? How might prayer, Bible study and intimacy with God make a difference?

Eight

The Magic Potion
That Tainted Our Fairy Tale

*Y*ou're the most beautiful woman in the world to me.
I cannot wait to marry you. I dream about all the
wonderful fights we will have. I relish the drama of being
kicked out of the bedroom. And then you can tell your parents
and your friends what a louse I am. Divorce court—that will
be a blast! Imagine all the sympathy we will get from our
friends. All you have to do is say yes."

What a proposal that would be! No one anticipates the
heartache that marriage often brings. The excitement and optimism of an engaged couple is amazing. They both believe that
their union will be harmonious to the end. I remember an
engaged friend who proclaimed, "We will never fight. We are
going to give each other back rubs every night!" Now, after ten

years of marriage, she chuckles at her naive expectations.

If a man and a woman both want an intimate and conflict-free marriage, why can't they just make it happen? Sure, there will be bumps along the road; perhaps debt, unemployment, illness or family problems. Some couples grow closer during difficult times. Others split apart with the slightest hint of stress. What makes the difference between the two?

There are a number of elements that, together, contribute to difficulty in close relationships. Not only is a wife dealing with her own issues, but her husband has his "sack of rocks" as well. The combination of life stresses and the emotional baggage of the bride and groom can be enough to quickly extinguish flames of love.

A Spell Has Been Cast

Tail of a lizard, tongue of a frog, liver of a cow, sap from the yucca plant, tooth of a dragon . . . These are the nasty ingredients that wizards and witches use in fairy tales to cast their evil spells. Sometimes it seems as if an evil potion of slimy ingredients has clipped the wings of lifelong commitment. Try as they might to promote intimacy, couples stumble under the influences of fears, doubts and insecurity. Before they know it, resentment, bitterness and the loss of hope have replaced their once unquenchable love and optimism.

An "evil spell" cast on marriages might include some of the following squalid ingredients.

The Impact of Early Experiences

Have you ever thought about what you do during the holidays? Do you put up a tree or a manger set? Do you hang stockings over the fireplace and put out cookies and milk for Santa? Do you wrap all of the presents? Do you put them out weeks before Christmas or Christmas night? Do you visit Grandma's house or a nursing home?

What do you usually do when you are sick? How do you care for your sick children? Do they get to watch TV? Do they drink chicken soup and eat pudding? Do they get to bring their pillow out on the couch or even sleep with Mom and Dad?

Just the smell of tapioca pudding reminds me of being sick. In fact, I can't remember ever eating it when I was healthy. I remember the first time I was sick as a married person. My husband suggested that I drink ginger ale. I thought he was nuts. Who drinks ginger ale when you are sick? Everyone knows that warm Coke settles the stomach.

There are many, many things that people do based on tradition. The way their parents did it is the way it is supposed to be done. This is not just true of Christmas traditions and illness rituals. The way people resolve conflict, how they handle anger, what they do to show love, how much they trust, what they expect their role in the family to be—the list goes on and on.

The effect of the past on the present is enormous. Many times this is good. There is no problem with washing the dishes the way Mom always did it. Why reinvent the wheel? However, some things people learn from the past can be problematic. This is particularly true when a person is unaware of the impact of the past.

There are two statements that everyone expects to hear from psychologists: "How do you feel about that?" and "Tell me about your mother." Although many of his theories are rather unsettling, Sigmund Freud emphasized a concept that is now universally accepted. People are deeply affected by the environment of their childhood.

Several theorists after Freud improved on this theory. Their work has been clumped together and termed "object relations theory." A basic understanding of the principles of object relations can help to explain why childhood relationships have so much impact on significant adult relationships.

A normal trait of childhood is called egocentrism. This means that kids view themselves as the center of the world. In fact, their young world revolves around them. They have difficulty understanding that others have emotions and thoughts apart from their own. Their teachers are not people, but teachers. They are not supposed to be in the grocery store or the mall, they belong in school!

I can remember the absolute astonishment I felt when I realized that all children did not have the same upbringing that I did. I remember my parents saying, "You are very blessed to have food on the table and parents who love you." Of course, but I did not believe reality existed apart from my world.

For this reason, Mom and Dad and other primary people in a child's life represent all people. Young minds form a basic understanding of themselves and others through their first significant relationships. Psychologists call these representations "objects."

Marge grew up in a home filled with conflict. Her mother was passive and always depressed. Her father was dominant and explosive. He ignored Marge and her siblings and became violent if they "got in his way." Marge's father seemed to believe that children were neither to be seen nor heard.

Through her earlier experiences, what kind of "objects" do you think Marge developed? Most likely she learned that she is not important. It is better for her to be silent and invisible. Her father represented males as hurtful, dominant and unfeeling. Her mother taught her that women are weak, defeated victims. Authority figures do not protect, but ignore and abuse their position.

Imagine how such preconceptions about herself, males and females will affect her marriage. Hopefully, Marge's later experiences will challenge some of these assumptions. However, what a child learns about herself and others is difficult to unlearn. Early childhood experiences are stored in the memory with emotions rather than words. A two-year-old may lack the words and understanding to remember that Dad yelled all the time. But the experience of feeling unsafe and unlovable will be permanently registered.

Object relations theory describes how those early relationship experiences are transferred onto current relationships. Marge will likely act toward her husband just like she acted toward her father. In fact, she may even seek a man with dominating traits similar to those of her father. People tend to gravitate toward familiarity, even if what is familiar is destructive. A woman like Marge may resist a relationship that challenges such assumptions as, "I am unworthy, unlovely and incapable." Even Marge's ability to trust God may be affected by her father's abuse of his authority. She may have great difficulty accepting God as loving and forgiving.

People have strong reactions to their painful early experiences. In fact, it is common for a man or a woman to marry someone who is the exact opposite of their parents. A good friend of mine grew up with a dominating and abusive mother. Her father was loving, but very passive. Her father could not protect her against the wrath of her mother. My friend consciously declared, "I will never marry a weak man who cannot protect me." Sure enough, her husband is anything but weak.

The impact of the models of early childhood cannot be overstated. This is particularly true of childhood experiences that have not been adequately processed and thought through. What is unconscious has a profound effect on the emotional decisions a person makes in relationships.

Adolescence (from about twelve years to twenty years in age) also represents a critical time in a person's development. The foundations of lifetime decisions are laid in this relatively short period of time. In particular, a young man or woman develops a sense of identity, which transcends his or her family. During the teen years, deeply held beliefs about competence, self-esteem and sexuality are formed.

Although parents continue to have a strong impact on an adolescent's development, experiences with friends and dating are also important. Many women (and men) have destructive experiences during these impressionable years. Examples include sexual abuse, consistent rejection and failure, sexual promiscuity and abortion. As they enter early adulthood, poor choices and tragic experiences may continue to shape their understanding of male-female relationships.

The impact of such negative early experiences leads to one common trait: fear. Intimacy is absolutely impossible in the context of fear. Intimacy, as explained earlier, requires that both husband and wife are willing to become vulnerable.

A woman who has been sexually victimized in the past may have incredible difficulty trusting her husband emotionally and sexually. His approaches to her will naturally result in fear and guardedness. A man who was abandoned by his first wife may live in fear of another rejection. He may be suspicious of any contacts his second wife has with other men and keep her isolated.

In many marriages, husbands and wives are beginning with the assumption of guilty until proven innocent. Every misunderstanding is laden with fears of repeated patterns from the past. They put on layers of protective armor, banishing all possibility of closeness. Soon the marriage resembles a war zone, with each spouse fighting for emotional survival.

There is a time to put the past away and focus on the present. Someone once said, "Past experience should be a guide post, not a hitching post." People who perpetually think about the past become victims of it. However, the opposite is also true. Ignoring the effects of the past can equally enslave a person's present decisions. It is vitally important to understand the people that influenced your life, and to become aware of how those experiences affect your current relationships.

Journaling, reading and talking about past experiences can be helpful. When very painful memories are involved, professional help may be important. Christian counselors and psychologists are trained in helping people understand and accept life experiences. Most importantly, they are committed to applying insight to changes in daily life.

Many people did not grow up in homes that modeled a healthy marriage. So how are these people supposed to know what good communication looks like? Where will they learn how to resolve an argument without screaming at each other? From watching *Ozzie and Harriet* reruns?

Discipleship and mentoring are excellent ways for a couple to learn what they may not have learned growing up. Choose a couple who is older than you and whose lives show a strong commitment to God and to marriage. Of course, mentors are only human. However, they can serve as wonderful role models and sources of information about real-life issues.

Misunderstanding People and Roles

A major stumbling block to healthy relationships is misconceptions about people and how they should relate. Over the past thirty years, pastors, psychologists, writers and speakers have done a wonderful job of providing resources filled with helpful information for husbands and wives. Seminars, books and counseling are excellent ways to learn about communication, conflict resolution, physical intimacy and other issues.

Even in the wake of all of this information, there are a few areas that continue to be misunderstood by large numbers of husbands and wives. In some cases, well-meaning leaders provide information that may be incorrect. The two areas that are most commonly misunderstood are biblical roles within marriage and self-esteem.

We have already covered the issues of submission, authority within marriage and biblical roles in previous chapters. Therefore, this discussion will be brief. Many Christian resources shy away from directly tackling this touchy debate. Submission and authority are words laden with controversy and emotion. However, misunderstanding biblical submission, a woman's power and a husband's authority are primary ingredients for disaster. These are very subtle dynamics that have a profound influence on the success of a marriage.

With the rise of popular psychology, many Christian leaders have denounced counseling and psychological principles. Their primary concern is the humanistic underpinnings of most psychological theories. The emphasis on self-esteem is a danger signal to many Christians. Servants of Christ are to be humbly aware of their inadequacies and depravity.

True, pride is a very dangerous quality. Pride led to Satan's rebellion and to Adam and Eve's sin in the Garden of Eden. In fact, a proud husband or wife will doom the fate of a marriage. However, there is a critical difference between pride and self-esteem.

Scripture is very clear that humans are not gods. People are fallen and sinful at heart. The Bible also clearly communicates that men and women are precious in God's sight. He cares for each one and sent His Son for each person individually. People are not perfect, but they are valuable.

It is very appropriate for a person to defend the value of her own life, choices and existence. In fact, it is critical to healthy relationships. Having a solid acceptance of self-esteem does not mean selfishness. Paradoxically, it is only through accepting God's love and value for oneself that a person can truly become a servant. A person who is convinced of her own worthlessness serves out of weakness, rather than choosing to serve out of love.

In an effort to discourage pride, some Christians believe they must under-emphasize their own value. They muddle through life mentally rehearsing phrases like, "My needs don't count. I am not important. If I can make people happy, then maybe I can be of some value." Imagine the impact this has on a marriage! This type of wife may encourage her husband to become more selfish. She is not a contributing partner, but a self-defeating martyr.

So, how does a person affirm self-worth while avoiding pride? Pride enters the picture when one of two things happen. First of all, a person with a good self-image understands that her value comes from God. He is the source of all worth. It is not talents, achievements or beauty that bring value, but the status of being created by God. The creation can never become more valuable than the Creator. Proud people believe that they have created their own value through their good works, achievements or even their "humility." At this point, they have become their own gods.

I recently heard a well-respected pastor say, "The problem with our society is our obsession with self-esteem." Our world is obsessed with self-esteem because it does not understand the true source of value. Once God is seen as the giver of all value, the question of self-worth is settled. In fact, true "self-esteem" is better termed "God-esteem."

Pride also is in play when a person does not recognize that every person has the same value as others. In college, I was wrestling with issues of self-esteem and self-worth. I have always been very achievement-oriented. In my heart, I believed that I was valuable primarily by being successful. I was desperate to please authority figures and to be the best. Through reading a wonderful book (*The Search For Significance*, by Robert Scott McGee), I realized that I have great value based solely on my status as God's creation and His love for me. What a revelation this was!

I distinctly remember washing my hands in a rest room and seeing a woman who was cleaning the toilets. Her appearance was shabby and dirty. Then it hit me. *This woman has the exact same worth before God as I do. She is every bit as valuable as I am.* A healthy understanding of self-esteem comes not only from understanding the high value that God has placed on me, I must also understand that he has placed that same value on every other person. It is impossible to become proud with that realization. In fact, it is this that leads to the desire to serve and love others.

Some people serve, hoping to find worth and acceptance through their actions. Usually, such individuals are angry and depressed at heart. True servants are selfless only after they realize the incredible value that God has given them and those around them. They no longer have to justify their existence or prove their worth. They are free to serve, knowing that God has already settled the matter.

An understanding and acceptance of self-esteem is essential to developing a healthy and intimate relationship. Depending on others to determine my worth creates a dependency that saps the strength out of any intimate relationship. In fact, it makes being vulnerable almost unbearable. If I give my husband the role of determining how valuable I am, then he can potentially destroy me. If I have accepted my worth based on my relationship with God, I can be vulnerable to sharing myself with my husband. His rejection will hurt, but it does not threaten my emotional survival. This allows me to serve my husband without depending on his reaction to validate my own worth.

Unrealistic Expectations

Friends and Lovers

"My husband and I just don't seem to be great friends. In fact, I am not sure I even love him!" Susan could not imagine being married under these conditions. In her mind, being married meant being the best of friends and feeling madly in love. The absence of these circumstances, therefore, meant the end of her marriage.

Although romantic love and a vibrant friendship are desirable in marriage, they are not defining qualities. They are often the *by-product* of a good marriage, but are not the *foundation.*

In the musical *Fiddler on the Roof,* Tevye asks his wife, Golde, "Do you love me?" Golde replies in song, "For twenty-five years I've washed your clothes, cooked your meals, cleaned your house, given you children, milked the cow. After twenty-five years, why talk about love right now?" He keeps asking, and finally she concludes, "I suppose I do."

Brides and grooms have not always had lofty expectations of marriage. In many cultures, the parents have arranged marriages for their children. Being married meant a lifelong commitment, sharing a home, having children, dividing responsibilities and learning to love each other.

Many positive results have emerged from expecting more from marriage. Good marital relationships can be extremely fulfilling and meaningful. However, the broadening of expectations has also contributed to the destruction of many unions. Even the most committed couple finds it difficult to fight the notion that marriage means feeling love and experiencing friendship. Husbands and wives increasingly depend on each other to meet all of their social, emotional and spiritual needs.

No one person can be everything to their spouse. It is vitally important for both husband and wife to continue to nurture other significant relationships with parents, siblings and friends. The expectations placed on marriage today are so cumbersome that enjoying and appreciating the relationship rarely occurs. Both husband and wife feel the constant pressure to provide more and to be more. They panic when their feelings of love and friendship waver.

Married people do not always share the same interests and hobbies. To some extent, they can learn to do this. However, there needs to be room for a man to play basketball with the guys and for a woman to have lunch with her friends. Clearly, God intended for the marriage relationship to be the most intimate and significant. However, he did not intend for it to be the only relationship.

I have thoughts and feelings that my husband may not fully understand. I have hobbies that he may not be particularly interested in. This leaves me three choices. I can forget about my interests. After a time, I may begin to resent the fact that I gave up so much of myself because of him. My second choice is that I can force him into participating. "Mike, I read this book and I really liked it. If you love me, you will read it and talk about it with me." Then, he will begin to resent me. My third choice is to seek another outlet for my interests. For example, I might join a book club.

After All, Men Are Only Human

Another fatal trap is when a wife expects her husband to meet needs that only God can meet. She depends on him to reassure her, encourage her and pull her through every difficulty of life. This is part and parcel of the fantasy of "the prince." At some level, she married him to be rescued. When her "hero" fails her, she feels betrayed and abandoned.

Certainly, everyone goes into marriage with expectations to receive something: companionship, love, identity, security, etc. However, the heart of marriage is the expectation of giving. Is it possible to give when you are not receiving? There are times in every marriage when a wife feels as if she is doing all of the giving and all of the serving. Her needs seem to be ignored.

As long as a wife depends upon her husband to meet her deepest needs for significance and security, her marriage is on tenuous ground. The moment her prince fails her, which he will, her commitment wavers. The strength and resolve of a godly wife comes through one thing: she depends on her Heavenly Father to meet her deepest needs. She will still work to improve her marital relationship, but her survival does not depend on her husband. She can walk the tightrope of intimacy without a safety net, because God is holding her hand. (*The Marriage Builder,* by Larry Crabb, is an excellent resource for women who find themselves in this situation.)

The Slickest One of Them All

Sexual abuse, poor parenting, a meddling mother-in-law . . . they all affect how wives interact with their husbands. There are always reasons why married people act in ways that destroy intimacy. However, there is no denying that sin plays an ugly and prominent role.

I Corinthians 10:13 states there is no temptation that a

Christian must give into. God always provides a way out of doing the wrong thing. As hard as it is to admit, many marriages are destroyed by plain old sin.

Of course, the obvious sins like adultery, drunkenness, lying and explosive tempers are prime examples. Some men seem to specialize in these. But the subtle, quiet sins of many wives play just as much havoc on the marriage relationship. Gossip, seething anger and hatred, selfish manipulation, keeping records of wrong, refusal to forgive—the painful list goes on and on.

Although there are many reasons for sin, there are no excuses. Every man and woman is confronted daily with countless opportunities to do the right thing or the wrong thing. The consequences may not be immediate, but they will be certain. I cannot eat a box of chocolate every day without it affecting my weight, cholesterol level and general health. The same is true with sin. Eventually, it will take its toll on the health of a marriage.

It is so easy to pick out what my husband is doing wrong. It is much more difficult to honestly address the sinful attitudes in my life that affect our marriage. I rationalize by saying, "If only he would do this, then I could do that." In reality, I do not want to serve unless I am being served. I feel justified staying in the role of a victim rather than addressing my contributions to the problem.

In many marriages, the wife truly feels like the victim. Her husband has made bad decisions time and time again. He refuses to give up his sinful lifestyle. Even in these situations, the wife may be contributing in very subtle ways. For example, her anger may be dictating every move she makes. In her heart of hearts, she may not want to help him get better because she is so angry with him.

Regardless of the situation, there are always temptations for a wife to contribute to a destructive dynamic—sometimes through her actions and sometimes through her unwillingness to act. She cannot change him, but she can be honest about her own part in their marital mess. This can go a long way in promoting reconciliation and change in their relationship.

Is There an Antidote?

Are we doomed to live under the awful spell of emotional baggage, unrealistic expectations and sinful temptations? Should we call the divorce lawyers now to get a jump on the inevitable? Discussing all of the things that can go wrong in a marriage can feel pretty hopeless.

One of the most profound statements I have ever read is from the book *The Road Less Traveled,* by M. Scott Peck. He explains that life is difficult. Once we accept that life is difficult, it becomes less difficult.

People spend so much time and energy trying to avoid pain that they end up living right in the middle of it. Growth, change and awareness can be quite painful. French philosopher La Rochefoucauld said, "Almost all of our faults are more pardonable than the methods we think up to hide them." Confronting sin in your life is no fun. Learning new ways of interacting with your husband can be frightening. Most people are too afraid of the risk and the pain to do these things.

Ironically, the more they avoid pain, the longer they live in it. Proverbs 8 talks about Wisdom, who cries out in the streets begging for people to listen to her. Some listen, but many choose the easy route. Day after day they remain in their folly. Solomon says the foolish are like a dog returning to its vomit. Eventually, Wisdom is silent. The foolish and the naive are left to live in the destruction of the easy road they have chosen. Proverbs 1:24–32 (NIV) says:

> *But since you rejected me when I called and no one gave heed when I stretched out my hand, since you ignored all my advice and would not accept my rebuke, I in turn will laugh at your disaster; I will mock when your calamity overtakes you—when calamity overtakes you like a storm, when disaster sweeps over you like a whirlwind, when distress and trouble overwhelm you. Then they will call to me, but I will not answer; they will look for me, but will not find me. Since they hated knowledge and did not choose to fear the Lord, since they would not accept my advice and spurned my rebuke, they will eat the fruit of their own ways and be filled with the fruit of their own schemes.*

These are very harsh words. They are also true words. For years, a woman has ignored warning signs of her husband's promiscuity. Another refuses to address the fears of past abuse in her life. Still another harbors feelings of bitterness and anger, all the while professing to being in God's will. The results are predictable. The time comes when it is too late for wisdom to bring healing and prevent destruction.

The question is this: what is more important? Staying "safe" and "comfortable" or becoming a godly wife? The choice is not an easy one. If your marriage is in a state of disarray, addressing the problems will be hard. Your resolve must be great. You must first decide two things: how important is your marriage and how committed are you?

I remember meeting with a woman who insisted that her marriage was hopeless. Over the course of many meetings, she learned how her own sin and poor choices were contributing to the destructive pattern. She insisted over and over that she was unable to change. Our work together ended when she acknowledged that it was not a matter of ability, but a matter of will. One of Satan's most seductive traps is convincing us that we *cannot* do what we *will not* do.

Over the past year, I have witnessed some truly miraculous changes in marriages. Yes, one or both parties were willing to address the problems. However, I cannot explain from a psychological perspective what has happened in the lives of these individuals. When it comes down to it, God can radically change lives! Even the hardest heart can be softened by the touch of God. He can tear down walls of anger, guilt and fear if couples become willing participants.

When a woman has done her part to promote change in her marriage, she must depend on God to do the rest. The power of her sincere prayers, however, cannot be overstated. It is the secret weapon!

Developing intimacy in a marriage is hard work. It never just happens. The steps mentioned above are disciplines. They take dedication, commitment and risk. However, they are essential to promoting an atmosphere in which intimacy can grow, even through life's greatest difficulties.

> *The wise woman builds her house, but with her own hands the foolish one tears hers down.*
>
> **Proverbs 14:1, NIV**

Questions for Discussion and Reflection

1. What did you learn about the role of a wife from your mother? What did you learn about the role of a husband from your father? How have those lessons affected your marriage, for better or for worse?

2. How have early experiences in your life affected how you view God? What truths about God do you struggle to accept as a result? What truths about yourself do you struggle to accept?

3. The Bible speaks very strongly about pride (read Proverbs 16:18, I John 2:16, and James 4:6). However, many verses highlight God's high value of men and women (read Matthew 10:29–31, John 3:16, I John 3:1, Luke 15:4–6). What is the difference between pride and self-esteem? True humility and false humility? Why is understanding this important to a healthy marriage?

4. Read Romans 7:18–24. Even when we desire to do what is right, we are naturally drawn toward sin. What sinful desires do you "wage war against" in your marriage? What can you do about this? (Read Psalm 139:23–24).

5. To what extent are the difficulties in your marriage due to an unwillingness to change rather than an inability to change? What can you do about your unwillingness? What can you do about your inability?

Nine

Husband-Proofing
the Home

When our oldest son was eight months old and became mobile, my husband and I faced the daunting task of child-proofing our home. Every outlet had to be covered, wires secured, cleaning products placed behind lock and key and anything fragile placed out of reach. We purchased two bottles of syrup of ipecac "just in case." Of course, the occasional bump and bruise could not be avoided. But so far, our vigilance has protected our little boy through the curious stages of the first three years of life.

While visiting friends and relatives, we often have the unpleasant experience of bringing a one-year-old and a three-year-old into a house that is not child-proof. Mike and I play man-to-man defense, trying to protect our host's crystal and porcelain decorations. It seems that every sentence is interrupted with, "Andrew, don't climb the stairs!" "Don't put that in your mouth!" or "Be gentle with that cat!" Life is much more peaceful for all of us when home is safe to roam without unreasonable dangers.

The parallel of "husband-proofing" a home is not meant to be patronizing. Men are capable of protecting themselves and their families from most physical threats. However, many homes contain snares and dangers of a different sort that can easily wound a man's confidence and feeling of security. It is not uncommon, in fact, for a man to avoid home at all costs. He may fear emotional dangers that seem to jump out of nowhere and make him feel like a failure in his own home. Work, church or community activities, a drink with the guys, almost anything is more comfortable than home can sometimes be.

Most wives plead to have their husbands home more. They wish them to be more attentive and "present," even when they are at home. They complain that the romantic men they married have become bumps on a log, incapable of any meaningful interaction. There are many reasons why men avoid home, but almost invariably their avoidance speaks of their discomfort.

People like to spend time where they feel wanted, useful, respected and capable. Men are no different. Is it any wonder that they often prefer their work to the minefield that home can be? In counseling, men sometimes confess how inadequate they feel in the realm of marriage and family. One man exclaimed, "I don't know what to do when she cries. I feel completely helpless!" "I can never do enough to make my family happy. They always seem to want more!" another husband lamented.

Just as electrical outlets and lamps are dangers for toddlers, there are predictable domestic perils for husbands. Fortunately, a sensitive and vigilant wife can avert many of these. She is capable of making her home a safer emotional place for her husband. Essentially, she can invite him to become the hero of their home.

Dodging Financial Fiascos

Credit card debt, bankruptcy, stinginess, greed, foolish decisions, poor planning and plain financial hardship can be frightening threats to a marriage. Although both husband and wife are involved in the household expenses, the husband usually bears the brunt of responsibility when creditors knock at the door. Financial problems of any kind can keep a man awake at night or running scared from the home.

The arena of money is something that I know little about. There are reams of wonderful books on the topic that far surpass this discussion. (See books from Christian Financial Concepts, founded by Larry Burkett, for more complete information about financial issues in marriage.) However, the relational aspect of money is an important element of a wife's support of her husband. A few principles can help avoid the devastating financial burden that so easily destroys a husband's confidence.

Respect the Emotions that Money Represents

At first glance, finances seem kind of boring. Budgets, expense reports, earnings—they are simply a bunch of numbers. However, there is more to money than meets the eye. Money is meaningful to people. In fact, it may hold unique meaning for every person in the family.

Dan grew up during hard financial times. His parents had to work very hard just to meet basic expenses. Throughout his childhood, there were many things that Dan was unable to do because of financial constraints. He was one of the only sixth-graders to miss the class trip to Washington, D.C. When his friends were going on dates and playing basketball, he worked two jobs. He wore his brother's worn-out clothes that always seemed to hang from his small frame. Remembering the disappointments and embarrassments of his past, Dan was committed to earning a good living as an adult. His children would want for nothing. He would spare no expense. His cars, clothes, home and luxuries would always exceed the standards of his peers.

Sheila, Dan's wife, viewed money very differently. She also grew up in a lower-middle-class home. Her father worked hard to earn a decent wage. However, Sheila's parents had not been careful with their money. After several ill-advised decisions, the family had lost their home. She remembered her parents fighting about money and wondering how they would provide for their family. To Sheila, money meant safety and security. As a young teen, she vowed to always be careful with her money and to spend only what was necessary.

By the time she met Dan, Sheila had accrued a modest

savings account. Dan noticed Sheila's frugal nature and loved to spoil her with the things she would never buy for herself. By the end of their first year of marriage, money had become a major source of conflict. To Dan, having nice things meant success and respect. To Sheila, it reflected recklessness.

Every time Dan made a lavish purchase, Sheila interpreted his actions as not caring about her fears. When Sheila pouted and nagged about Dan's spending, he saw her deliberately standing in the way of his happiness. Neither of them were trying to hurt the other. They were defending their own emotional turf. Regardless of their motives, the end result was hostility and tension.

It is impossible to successfully navigate the mire of money in a marriage without understanding what it symbolizes for each person. Why is the husband motivated to save while the wife cannot spend it fast enough? Money represents very strong fears and drives. When a husband or wife ignores the emotional side to money, they can be pouring salt in an open wound. Every financial decision is also an emotional one.

A Team Approach

There are several reasons why one person in the marriage naturally gravitates towards financial tasks. Sometimes one is just better at numbers. Maybe the wife has more time, or the husband believes it is a man's job. Perhaps he can only feel at rest if he knows where every penny is spent. Or maybe she just does not trust him.

Although one person must be responsible for actually

writing the checks, both the husband and wife need to be involved in the finances. There are many reasons for this. Both should be aware of the family's financial matters in case one of them is incapacitated. Two different perspectives on money can help keep the family financially balanced. Both the husband and wife need to feel that their interests and concerns are being addressed. A team approach to finances also takes the brunt of responsibility off one person. Perhaps most importantly, it provides an aspect of accountability.

Often in counseling, a wife is devastated to learn that her husband has fallen thousands of dollars into debt over the years. She may be shocked to find that he has burned through their savings for retirement by gambling on high-risk investments. A husband may be furious when he discovers that he cannot take out a loan because of the credit card debt his wife has secretly accumulated. All of these scenarios could have been avoided with a team approach.

First, the husband and wife together need to agree on a budget and financial guidelines for their family. Perhaps with the help of a financial counselor, this may involve several discussions formulated over a few months. Budgets and planning must be revisited periodically as needs and circumstances change.

Second, the couple should regularly review their budget, credit card statements and general expenses. Financial software for home computers makes this task easier than it used to be. Powerful programs like Quicken provide detailed reports about income and spending that are user friendly. Although this requires a time commitment, it prevents full-blown marital schisms due to financial problems. It is a wise investment.

Make Financial Decisions Beforehand

As a teenager in a Christian school, I heard countless speeches and sermons on sexual purity. One primary piece of advice was to always set your moral standards before a date, not while on the date. The principle is that while in the "heat of the moment," your judgment is not likely to be sound.

The same is true of finances. Money problems are often due to impulsive spending. In fact, sales people make a living based on impulsive purchases. They are trained to encourage a consumer to buy without thinking, planning or consulting.

A couple tosses around the idea to buy a new car, as their old one is becoming unreliable. They take a Saturday to visit some dealerships. They have done little research on cars, have not discussed what they can afford and are not planning to buy a car that day. Naively, they walk into the first dealership, and immediately an enthusiastic sales person pounces on them. Within five minutes, they are test driving a top-of-the-line model. Leather seats, CD player, power everything. What luxury! The looks on their faces tell the whole story. The couple begins to leave for the next dealership. Not wanting to lose the sale, the sales person reminds them that the special rebate deal is only good for today. Within an hour, the couple has signed the papers and committed to a car that is far beyond their means.

Weeks later, they realize the financial bind they are in. What seemed to be such a good decision has severely limited their financial freedom for years to come. If they had committed to a certain figure before they began their shopping or had left their checkbook at home, their problem may have been avoided.

Setting a budget together also allows for violations of the budget to be clearly addressed. The budget becomes the "bad guy." Marcy and Jim had agreed to spend $600 total on Christmas presents ($300 for each). Marcy spent her $300. Jim went a little overboard, spending more than $500 on his friends and family. Naturally, they exceeded their budgeted amount. Marcy was quite upset at Jim for his indulgences. Because they had agreed on $600, she could say to him, "Do you remember what we had budgeted for Christmas? I am upset that you broke the agreement we made."

Their decision had been mutually agreed upon. Therefore, their commitment, not Marcy, served as the standard. Had they not talked about the budget ahead of time, Marcy would likely never have addressed Jim about his spending. She probably would have harbored her resentment without ever knowing how to bring it up. If she had, Jim may have viewed her as nagging him over some arbitrary amount of money that represented "too much."

Money can be used to send strong emotional messages. Unfortunately, few couples honestly decode those messages and talk about the conflicts that their financial behavior represents. Money symbolically then becomes a primary source of anger and resentment. Planning is often effective in clarifying the relational aspects that may be involved in spending.

Each Person Needs Some Financial Freedom

Although financial decisions should be made together, it is also important for both the husband and wife to have some of their "own" money.

A wife wants to be able to go out to lunch without feeling guilty about it. Her husband likes expensive coffee. She reminds him that his $3 latte can be made at home for 15 cents. Even if it is a minimal amount, personal money should be budgeted for each person that can be spent any way they want—no guilt, pressuring or questions. It is amazing how much a little bit of freedom can take the edge off financial strain of a marriage.

This is particularly important if a husband and a wife have different financial philosophies. Dan and Sheila, who are mentioned, are a great example of this. It is important for Dan to have some money to buy the things that are important to him. If Sheila keeps him from this, he will surely be resentful. On the other hand, it is important for Sheila to feel financially responsible and secure. Their needs seem to be mutually exclusive. Here is a solution that will allow both of them to be reasonably comfortable.

Dan and Sheila agree that their living expenses and tithe should be met first (this takes care of 80 percent of their after-tax income.) In addition, they agree to save 10 percent of their income. That leaves 10 percent surplus. They each get 5 percent to do whatever they want. If Dan wants to buy a designer suit, fine. If Sheila cuts out coupons and sews her own clothes to save money, she can invest the extra for security. Dan never questions Sheila, and Sheila never questions Dan. Dan is satisfying his need to enjoy what he earns without compromising his wife's need for stability.

Some couples even go so far as to have separate accounts. This allows the frugal one to save every penny and prevents the spendthrift from buying more with the resulting savings.

Although this solution may seem divisive (my money and your money), it can bring unity by resolving a constantly contentious battle.

Avoiding Failed Fathering

"Scott, I have wonderful news! We are going to have a baby!" Cindy could not be more excited. She had dreamed for years of this moment. She and her husband were going to be parents in just eight months.

Cindy enthusiastically prepared their home for the new arrival. The den became a nursery with pastel wallpaper and an antique white crib. She shopped for little sleepers, blankets and booties. After each purchase, she gleefully paraded her treasures for Scott. As Cindy's belly expanded, she reveled in the identity of "Mom." She read parenting books, took classes on natural childbirth, breast-feeding, infant care and anything else that would help her become more prepared for her child's arrival.

Scott's life did not change much throughout the pregnancy. There were no showers for him at work or helpful advice from veterans. He just received a pat on the back when his baby girl, Megan, was born. Although delighted to be a father, Scott harbored fears about providing financially and emotionally for his growing family. At thirty, he still felt like a boy pretending to be his daddy.

Cindy seemed to adjust so well. Sure, she had been weepy a few nights and called her mother for advice when Megan was sick. But she had become a pro at handling this precious little life. In fact, she seemed consumed by her new role of mother.

It was six months before Scott could convince her to leave Megan for an evening to have dinner alone. Sex became a very rare occurrence. Even when they were "away" from their baby, Cindy constantly talked and worried about her. Scott and Cindy seemed to have trouble connecting anymore. Although he didn't want to admit it, part of him began to resent his daughter for what she seemed to have taken from his marriage.

Scott's difficult transition into fatherhood is typical of what many husbands face. Although the life of a new child is cause for celebration, it also means important adjustments for a couple. A mother's obsession and infatuation with her child often comes at the expense of intimacy with her husband. The problems begin in infancy, but can sow seeds of disharmony that last the life of a marriage.

Make Sure He Doesn't Become Number Two

The experience of being a mother is one like no other in the world. Having that little life depend on you and love you can be so fulfilling. Later, soccer games, Christmas pageants, birthday parties and teacher's meetings fill the calendar. As time progresses, the challenge of guiding an adolescent through the teen years becomes all-consuming. Both the demands and the returns of motherhood can be phenomenal. The love a mother has for her child is perhaps the strongest emotion that a person experiences. Although it is a different kind of love, many women confess that they feel more bonded with their children than with their husbands. Where does this leave him? He may feel like the outsider. It seems impossible for him to break into the special bond of feelings that the mother and children have formed.

It is normal for a woman to be consumed by her infant for the first few months of the baby's life. It is also normal for a new dad to feel neglected during this period of time. However, as the days wear on, the priority of the marriage over the children must begin to find a balance. As children become a little less demanding and a little more durable, there must be time set aside for mom and dad to remember that they are first husband and wife.

If the priority of marriage is not reestablished, a woman can easily fall into the trap of depending upon her children to meet her emotional needs. She can look to them for comfort, companionship and reassurance. This has devastating effects both on parenting and marriage. She can justifiably be so involved in meeting her child's needs that she rationalizes ignoring her husband's. This is so easy to do!

More than once over the past few years, Mike has told me that he feels like he is getting "the leftovers." After taking care of the kids, work and household chores, I have little left for him. Even during times that we are alone, I am prone to run to the boys as soon I hear a whimper out of one of them. Sometimes I have to force myself to regularly schedule date nights and occasional weekend getaways. I want to spend time with my husband, but my kids' needs are so much more obvious. They seem so vulnerable and dependent upon me. I have to remind myself, however, that our marriage will wither away if we do not tend to it. Our love quickly turns to irritation and skepticism if we have not spent time talking, sharing and planning. I also must remember that neglecting our relationship makes us both more vulnerable to the attention of other admirers.

Give Him the Gift of His Child's Love

Counselors sometimes refer to the mother as the "switchboard." Every communication seems to go through her. "Mom, Amy is teasing me," her daughter complains. "Amy, stop teasing Angela," Mom intercedes. When the kids get older, the mom can still be the go-between. "Larry, I think Cheryl was hurt that you did not go to her house for Easter."

Mothers constantly find themselves interpreting and communicating between fathers and their children. A teen's mother will likely explain his father's curt response to the boy's request to use the car. "Your dad had a bad day. I'll talk to him about it when he calms down and maybe he will change his mind."

A mother's role as switchboard gives her a large amount of influence in the relationship of her children and husband. In many cases, children see and understand their fathers through the eyes of their mothers. By the time most children reach adulthood, they may view their fathers largely in the light of their mother's interpretations.

"Mommy, where is Daddy? Why can't he have a tea party with me?" a little girl asks. Most moms respond to this kind of question without even a second thought. How she responds over time to such questions will have an irreversible impact of this girl's view of her daddy. A neutral response may be, "He's at work, Honey." If she is angry at her husband, she might say, "Daddy is never home. He's always out working chasing down his dreams!" A thoughtful wife can frame her answer in a way that builds up her husband by saying, "I know Daddy would love to have a tea party with you, but he goes to work so we can have food, a home and clothes to wear. Maybe we can plan to have a tea party with him tonight."

Think about the differences of those three responses. All three of them probably reflect reality. Daddy has both altruistic and selfish reasons for working hard. The ones that are reinforced by his wife will become the reasons that his child remembers. What a powerful responsibility God has given to wives to shape the lifelong father-child relationship. A mother's influence is not felt by drastic, rare statements, but by the daily ways that she reflects her love, respect, anger or fear of her husband to her children.

One woman shared a memory that symbolized the love with which her mother spoke of her father. One year, her father gave her mother a harp for Christmas. When she opened the gift, the mother exclaimed to the children, "Do you know how many hours your father worked to buy me this harp? This is the most precious gift I have ever received!" Even as an adult, that woman remembers a picture of a loving, generous father.

A mother can teach her children to hate a loving father or to love an inadequate father. Over time, her perspective often becomes a self-fulfilling prophecy. Why should a man continue to try when he has already been declared a failure? Why would he give up when the ones he loves treat him like a hero?

I am extremely grateful for the relationship my mother

nurtured between my father and me. As a self-employed businessman, my dad traveled often. During my childhood, he was frequently out of town. My mom did a wonderful job of communicating Dad's loving intentions; I never questioned his absence. I remember our time together as frequent and special.

One day recently, my dad spontaneously stated, "I must be the happiest man on the face of the earth. Do you know why I am so happy?" he asked me. "Because all of my six children love me. Your mother gave me that gift," he said with a tear in his eye.

Help Him to Become a Competent Father

Let's face it. Most women are better at mothering than are their husbands. They know what to feed kids, know about bedtimes, know how to comfort when a child cries and seem to be aware of every possible danger facing a child.

Once I became a mother, I was amazed at how often women compare "mothering" notes. Bible studies, at the park, on the phone, at the grocery store—everywhere I went, I felt I was in a giant support group of mothers who were all experiencing similar stresses. The church offered classes, and bookstores were filled with books of helpful advice. Over time, I naturally have become an "expert" on caring for my children. My husband does not have this advantage. He has no idea that raisins cause diarrhea, that teething babies drool, that kids get hyperactive when they are anxious, that teens can't tell you when they are sad.

The exposure mothers have to child-rearing tools and

information is vital to the job of parenting. However, it also can put dads at a disadvantage.

A well-meaning father is playing with his five-month-old baby. He jiggles her, shakes her and throws her in the air. Mom sees their playtime and remembers the dangers of shaking a baby. She immediately corrects Dad. So the dad moves on to his seven-year-old child. They are playing catch with a football. The boy drops the ball and the father playfully responds, "Come on, butterfingers! You are playing like a sissy!" Mom has recently read that such words can be devastating to a young man's self-esteem. She scolds her husband for his insensitive remarks.

Poor Dad! He was trying to bond with his kids and fell flat on his face at each effort. Eventually, he gives up. He returns to reading his newspaper where he will not do any damage.

Here is the dilemma for every mother: How do you help your husband succeed as a parent without discouraging him with your criticism and humiliating him with constant advice? Here are three simple steps that can go a long way in achieving this goal.

1. *Let some things go.* There are many things in parenting that can be critical to a child's safety and development. However, there are other things that are just not that important. If every once in awhile Dad feeds David a food that is not good for him, it is not that big of a deal. If he puts Sara's bow in crooked and her dress does not match her shoes, who cares? If the dishes are not done when you come home from a night out, cut him some slack.

When you are bothered by something your husband is doing with the children, ask yourself how important it is in the long run. If it is not a big deal, ignore it. This will heighten the importance of your interventions when something really does matter. It will also drastically decrease the negative feedback your husband receives when he plays with the kids.

2. *Always thank and encourage him when he interacts with the kids.* All of us respond so much better to positive feedback than criticism. Even if your husband has done ten things wrong with the kids, highlight the one thing he did right. Bring it up over and over again. Let him know how much you appreciate his effort and how much his love means to the kids.

3. *Make someone else the expert.* As a mom, you have important information that can be very helpful to your husband as a father. He is much more likely to accept that information if it does not come directly from you (or from your mother!).

"Bob, what are you doing? Don't give Jimmy pizza right after he just threw up!" Bob is likely to walk away in disgust and say, "Well then, you feed the kids dinner!" This same scenario can be handled in a way that does not humiliate and discourage Bob. "Honey, thanks for trying to feed the kids dinner. I know you didn't know this, but Jimmy has had the flu. The doctor gave us this list of foods that would be good for his stomach."

There are many ways to make someone else the expert. Reading books together, attending classes together, at a neutral time discussing parenting tips you have learned can all help equip your husband without making him feel like a failure.

The Shadows of Superman

It's a bird, it's a plane, no—it's Superwife! Like Martha Stewart, she throws a dinner party for twelve without breaking a sweat. Every meal at her home has five delicious, nutritious, fat-free courses. She makes her own curtains and grows her own herbs. Not to mention that she works from home, earning a six-figure salary, while caring for her five perfectly-behaved, home-schooled children. Would you like to live next door to this woman?

I often bemoan the beautiful models that fill the pages of magazines, billboards and television screens, their faces flawless, each feature brimming with beauty and seduction. Their figures are perfectly proportioned without a hint of cellulite, stretch marks or varicose veins. I am careful to remind Mike that the pictures in magazines have been airbrushed. The models have starved themselves, have personal trainers, have fans blowing their hair perfectly. But who am I fooling? They are beautiful!

Although men and women are different in many ways, this is a similarity that they share. Men are as humiliated and defeated by perfection as women are. A wife's admiration and respect for the "perfect" husband down the street is as irksome to him as the Victoria's Secret catalog is to her. He becomes painfully aware that he does not fulfill her like another man could. He is not her hero.

As beautiful as models may be, their images in the media do not exactly reflect reality. They have a staff of people who are employed to make them look beautiful. Their two-dimensional images may be perfect, but no one sees the pain, insecurities and weaknesses of these "pictures of perfection."

The same is true of the men whom women often elevate to the status of superheroes. From a distance, a woman observes that such a man can do no wrong. He always seems loving to his family, provides a good income and charms everyone. Wistfully, a wife wonders how her life might be different if she had met this Prince Charming years ago. Surely she would not be buried in piles of laundry, in a dingy house, with screaming kids, if only. . . . She glances over at her husband who is sitting in his recliner, eating chips and watching baseball. Her discontent grows by the minute.

In reality, the revered superhero is probably not that super. He has flaws and imperfections of which only his discontented wife is probably aware. Superheroes are always destructive to a marriage. Poor Clark Kent! He and Lois Lane would likely have made a wonderful couple before Superman came around. However, after the man in tights saved her life, Lois had no interest in a mere mortal.

Superheroes can come in any shape or form. The suave, muscled hunk at the gym, the adoring father of five down the street, the successful doctor from church. Some women idolize their pastors.

A colleague of mine told me an interesting story years ago. She was working with a woman who was very discontent in her marriage. The client continually talked about how wonderful her pastor was. On and on she droned about how much better her life would be if only she had married a man like her pastor. Ironically, the pastor's wife started therapy a few months later, due to her own marriage problems with that same "perfect" husband.

Fathers can also take the role of a superhero, particularly for young women. *Dad.* The word is wonderful to someone who has a caring, protective father. The only problem with having a great dad is the concern that no man will be able to match him. A woman who has this concern usually passes a greater version of it to her husband.

Joanne had been blessed with a super dad. He was hard-working, sensitive and attentive. He would give anything for his little girl. Joanne and her dad had always enjoyed a special bond. Even through the awkwardness of adolescence, her respect and love for her father was evident.

One day, the inevitable happened. Joanne fell in love. Brad's charming personality, ambition and wit won her heart within a few months, and the young couple married shortly after. With tears in his eyes and a lump in his throat, her father walked Joanne down the aisle to her new life. He was so proud of her. He believed she could do anything. He liked Brad, but secretly worried that this young man was too immature to take care of his precious little girl.

Joanne and Brad rented an apartment just ten minutes away from the bride's family. The couple experienced the normal stress and conflict of newlyweds. A few times, their arguments were heated. Brad turned stone silent when he was angry. Joanne could not understand why he clammed up in the middle of an argument. He was so immature! Not like her father. In fact, sometimes it seemed that he did not care about her feelings.

When she felt discouraged, Joanne would sometimes jump into her beat-up car and drive to the safety and comfort of her childhood home. She and her dad would have tea and talk about her dilemma. Her father always wanted to help. Throughout their marriage, Joanne's father offered financial assistance, job references for Brad, good advice, a shoulder to cry on. He was Joanne's refuge.

Although Brad appreciated the intentions of his father-in-law, something inside him also resented this man. Brad felt like a child still trying to court Joanne. He believed he would never be good enough, old enough, stable enough and rich enough to take care of her. Brad knew that Joanne admired her father more than she admired anyone else. It was he that she ran to when she hurt or was in need.

A wonderful dad is truly a blessing from God. But the relationship between a parent and child must change with time. The protection, nurturing and direction of a godly parent in childhood can interfere with the bonding of marriage if it continues in adulthood.

Whatever form they may take, superheroes pose a serious threat to a marriage. As long as the dream and vision of a superhero lives on, a normal man has no chance of winning the heart of his wife. Her longings for someone greater constantly reminds him of his inadequacies, of the little boy that can never grow into a man. As long as a woman pours her energy into a fantasy, she destroys any hope of finding the hero in her husband. In fact, she stomps on his hope of becoming worthy of her love and respect daily.

Lackluster Leadership

One of the greatest paradoxes in marriage is a wife's desire to have her husband lead her, and her unwillingness to follow him when he does. Countless times in counseling, a strong, dominant woman complains that her husband never takes the initiative. Startled, her husband stares at her as if to say, "Yeah, right. Like you need a leader!"

Wives rarely realize how often they send these mixed messages. Perhaps this is because many women are not sure what they want. When a man takes the leadership of a home, his wife is likely to have two simultaneous responses. At one level, she is relieved to see her husband's strength. But she may also fear the loss of her independence and will. While begging him to take headship, she may also be sabotaging his every effort to do so. What a no-win situation for husbands!

Keep Yourself from Filling the Void

Something that often keeps a husband from stepping into a leadership role is that his wife is doing such a great job of taking charge. Without realizing it, a wife can assume the responsibility of making decisions and initiating in the family. There is no need for her husband to step up to the plate.

In some cases, a woman may be even more capable of leading than her husband. This is often true of spiritual leadership in the family. Many husbands feel dreadfully ignorant of spiritual issues compared to their wives. She knows how to pray better, reads the Bible more and knows all of the Bible stories. Her husband feels so insecure that he shies away from spiritual matters. In his absence, she takes the initiative. The more she leads the family, the more insecure he feels.

A husband will rarely step out as the head of the family if he feels less adequate than his wife. The trick is for a woman to use all of her strength, experience and knowledge to equip her husband to lead. She is a resource for him, not a replacement. She is his able teammate, not his daunting competitor.

There are some cases which demand that a wife step into a leadership role in the absence of her husband's initiative. However, most of the time, wives assume leadership out of their own fear and anxiety rather than out of necessity. One of the most difficult distinctions a wife must make is knowing when to be "silent" and when to "speak." This critical decision over time can have a powerful impact on her husband's willingness to assume his God-given role of leadership in the family.

Respond to His Initiative

Imagine going into Victoria's Secret and purchasing a revealing negligee as a surprise for your husband. He has told you that he needs you to be more sensual with him. You believe this to be a step in the right direction.

Your face reddens as you bring the item to the counter. After paying the clerk, you immediately stuff the bag into your purse. When you return home, you sneak your purchase past the kids and hide it in a dresser. Days go by before you muster up the courage to try it on. You lock the door and slip on the garment. Looking in the mirror, you feel absolutely ridiculous.

Weeks later, the kids are gone for the night and you decide the time has come to give your husband his gift. You are ready for a night of romance. After cooking a special dinner, you quickly shower and put on the dreaded apparel. You hear your husband pull up from work, peek out the window to make sure it is him and wait on the staircase for the pleased look on his face.

Your heart races as he walks through the door. He glances up at you and says, "Hi, hon. What's for dinner?" You walk closer to him, just in case he happened to miss what you were wearing. "Oh, nice outfit. Go put your robe on so we can have dinner," he says matter-of-factly.

Your husband has not said one bad word to you, but his indifference has absolutely humiliated you. You have taken an incredible risk because you wanted to please him. Your act of love made you vulnerable to a painful rejection. "Does he think I am wearing this for my health?" you ask yourself. Chances are slim that you will ever take such a risk again.

Strange as it may sound, taking leadership in a family is a similar risk for many husbands. He must gather his courage to step out with his thoughts, ideas and beliefs. He knows that he will bear the brunt of responsibility if his leadership fails. He knows that he will then be viewed as a failure—the ultimate humiliation.

When a husband leads, he may feel emotionally naked. His wife's response to his initiative is very important to his confidence and his willingness to take such risks in the future. It does not take hurting words to make leadership a bad experience. Casual indifference can make him feel foolish and ineffective.

As a newlywed, I had expressed to Michael how much I would love him to be the spiritual leader of our family. We decided that every Sunday we would make a point of praying together. One Sunday, shortly after we made this commitment, we were at my parent's house getting ready to watch a Miami Dolphins playoff game. Five minutes before kickoff, Mike pulled me aside and said, "Let's go into a private room and pray together."

"Now? We're going to miss the game!" I protested. "Let's do it later," I said, walking away. We had all day to pray and the big game was about to start. Why did he have to pick right now!

Mike's countenance fell immediately. He walked away feeling defeated and frustrated. I do not remember what happened to the Dolphins that day, but I do remember that I did not enjoy the game very much. Later we discussed the situation. Mike told me how frustrated he felt that I had not responded to his leadership. The experience had discouraged him from wanting to take the initiative again.

Particularly early in the relationship, a wife's response to her husband's attempts at leadership is critical. His ideas and decisions will not be perfect. However, if she wants him to be a confident leader for their family, she must encourage his willingness. Leading is a risk. It exposes the most vulnerable fears of a husband—failure and humiliation.

Encourage Him to Lead the Way He Leads

Some years ago, my parents were moving. I was off school for a few weeks and offered to help them pack. My parents had lived in that house for more than ten years and had accumulated lots of "stuff." My job was to help my mother pack boxes. The first day, I worked on the kitchen. About every two hours, my mom stopped into the kitchen to monitor my progress. Invariably, she was unhappy with the way that I packed something. Several times she asked me to unpack and repack a box entirely. By the end of the day, I was about to resign my position as "boxer." My mom picked up on my frustration and we talked about it over dinner.

"I can't help you unless you let me pack my way!" I exclaimed. "Why don't you just pack them yourself if you want everything to be so specific?" She got the point and apologized for micro-managing. "Okay. I promise not to check up on you anymore. I trust you to do a good job." For the next several days, we worked together without a hitch. Perhaps to my mom's surprise, all of her flatware, china and decorations were transported safely.

There is nothing more discouraging than having someone critique your every move. It communicates a lack of trust and confidence that is absolutely defeating. This is exactly what some wives do to their husbands. They not only ask him to lead, but insist on how he should lead.

This was a hard lesson for me to learn. As I noted in previous chapters, Mike and I have very different personalities. I was the person in school who finished a term paper weeks before it was due. Mike, on the other hand, pulled all-nighters.

His way of doing things stresses me out. I am convinced he will forget to pay a bill or follow through on a commitment. But you know what? He has his own way and his own timing of getting things done. He is a very capable leader, even if he does not do things the way I think they should be done. A wise counselor advised me early in our marriage to trust the way Mike operates, even if it does not make sense to me.

Home can be either the safest or the most dangerous place for a man. Nowhere is he more at risk. A husband's vulnerabilities provide the opportunity for a wife to either build or destroy his trust and confidence. Discovering the hero in your husband is a lifetime ambition. A wife's subtle efforts to make home a safe and encouraging place for him will, over time, make an extraordinary difference in the man that he becomes.

The wise woman builds her house, but with her own hands the foolish one tears hers down.

Proverbs 14:1, NIV

Questions for Discussion and Reflection

1. What emotional meaning does money hold for you? What does it mean to your husband? How have differences in money created conflict in your marriage? What practical changes in the way you approach money could improve your marriage?

2. Think about the last month. How has your attitude and speech toward your husband affected your children's view of him? How can you give your husband the gift of your children's love?

3. Are there any men in your life that have the status of superhero? Do you ever compare your husband to other men? How might this affect the chance for intimacy in your marriage?

4. Why is taking leadership often a big risk for a husband? What can you do (or not do) to encourage your husband to take this risk?

5. Ask your husband to rate on a scale from one to ten how confident he feels in these areas: finances, leadership and parenting. Then write down practical steps that you can take to bolster whatever area was the lowest.

Ten

Making Dreams Come True

What do you want to be when you grow up?" Troy's uncle asked him. The eight-year-old thought about it and replied, "Either an astronaut or a lion tamer." Boys and girls are taught to begin dreaming at a young age. In childhood, their dreams have no limit. A scrawny, short kid can imagine playing linebacker for the Dallas Cowboys. A little girl who stammers and stutters is a Supreme Court Justice when she closes her eyes. The possibilities are endless.

As the years pass, children turn into adolescents and then young adults. With each day, their dreams fade in the face of reality. Ten years later, eighteen-year-old Troy realizes that he will never be an astronaut or a lion tamer. He settles for working in the same factory in which his father has worked all of his life. Maybe Troy was able to hold onto a small fraction of his dream of being daring, brave and adventurous. However, he would never share his dream with anyone, fearing the humiliation as much as lamenting his failure to achieve it.

In my opinion, the best movies are true stories about people who believed in their dreams. *Rudy* is one of my favorites. It is about a young boy who grows up loving Notre Dame football. His dream is to play for the Fighting Irish. He triumphs over all odds trying to make his dream come true.

I saw this movie several years ago with some friends. A few said, "How stupid! This kid spent years of his life trying to achieve a childhood dream that really means nothing. Why would playing for a college football team be so important?"

What I love about this movie is that it expresses something central to the human soul. Dreaming is so important! I believe that our dreams are a key aspect to understanding God's work in our lives. God gives us each different passions. Sometimes dreams only seem to frustrate us when they do not come true. Other times, dreams motivate us beyond "reasonable" limits.

I am convinced that we all still have dreams. Our dreams may be buried deeply beneath years of discouragement, failure and humiliation. In fact, we might not acknowledge that we ever had a passion for life. Dreaming can be very dangerous. How can we be happy with today when our dreams are so unfulfilled? Better to be content and passionless than discouraged by a vision of what can never be.

A marriage can have only as much passion as the people within the marriage have. If their dreams are dead and their excitement has been extinguished, their marriage is likely to be dull and lifeless. Dreams are part and parcel of the people that make them up. A women's dreams are clearly important to her happiness and enthusiasm. Likewise, a man can never feel confident in his marriage if his dreams are not understood and supported.

Later in this chapter, I will speak briefly about how both a husband's and wife's dreams can be validated within a marriage. However, the majority of our time will be spent discussing how to nurture your husband's dream. This is not meant to discount the importance of a wife's dream. That topic deserves a book of its own! The purpose of this book is to inspire women in their pursuit of godly, growing marriages. Encouraging a husband's dream is a vital aspect in this endeavor.

The Daily Grind

For most men, the fulfillment of their dream or the lack of its fulfillment boils down to one word: *work.* For the fortunate man, work is the fulfillment of his dream. What he does is directly connected to his passions and vision. Unfortunately, this is a rare occurrence. Even in a free society in which a person can pursue any occupational course, many men work at jobs that have little to do with what gets them excited about life.

Much of a man's life takes place outside of his home. He spends more time working than doing anything else besides sleeping. Over half of his waking time is spent toiling away at "the daily grind." After he clocks out of the office, he clocks into work around the house or in the community. His weekends quickly fill up with yard work, household projects and coaching Little League. When he is not working, he is usually thinking about work—or at least plotting how to avoid it! A man's life revolves around work.

Work is often the centerpiece of a man's life. Therefore, it is almost impossible to have a peaceful, contented environment in a marriage if a husband has significant job-related struggles. His work not only affects his life, it has a profound effect on the family. A wife can feel helpless in the middle of his depression and complaining. After all, what can she do to make his work go smoothly? How can she help him feel successful outside the home?

For a wife, her husband's work can be a tremendous source of frustration and stress. Of course, his job may be the sole or main source of income for the family. Equally stressful, however, is the impact work may have on her husband. It is such a big part of his life that it is difficult for him to feel dynamic, content and confident if work is not going well. As is true in many aspects of marriage, his frustration quickly becomes hers as well. Comments that I have heard women make about their husband's work include:

- "Bob will never be happy in his job. He constantly complains about work."
- "I cannot get Jim to do anything around the house. He's so lazy!"

- "Sam works constantly. I feel like our family does not even matter to him."
- "I wish Will would get a real job."
- "Jack has no people skills. He's destined to lose every job he gets."
- "Matt has been depressed ever since he retired."
- "John is obsessed with earning money."

The first step towards helping your husband in this endeavor is understanding the meaning of work in his life. He may feel trapped in a career that he does not like, or in which he finds no significance. He may face a boss who belittles and humiliates him every day. He may question his own competence and ability. He may feel one day away from failing or being fired. Work is stressful and very frustrating. A wife must realize this if she wants to truly be his partner.

The Meaning of His Work

Women work, too—some primarily in the home and others at professional careers. Although a woman may enjoy and value her job, work usually takes on a different level of importance for men. For the average man, work is a vital validation of his worth. To fail at work is to fail as a man. Even if a career-minded wife may understand her husband's drive to succeed, she likely underestimates the force of this drive.

When two men are introduced, the first thing they ask each other is "What do you do?" Immediately, the two size each other up. Who has the better job? Who is more powerful? Who is more successful? Who is more important? It is hard for a woman to understand how important work is for a man. It is his identity, his significance and his life.

Interestingly, many last names have been derived from the work that ancestors once performed. Years ago, it was Jim the blacksmith, Sam the baker, Tom the cook and George the fisher. In truth, men are still identified by what they do. It defines them in the world's eyes. No wonder work causes so much pressure for husbands. Their emotional survival and social standing often seem to depend on their work status. Even while performing a worthwhile task that provides a healthy income, a man can feel like a failure next to someone who has more prestige or earns more money.

Men are driven by far more than money when it comes to working. In fact, money is simply symbolic of how valuable a man is to society. It is not the money that counts, it is what that money communicates. If a man drives a Mercedes and wears designer suits, he must be powerful, successful and important. Anywhere he goes, people will treat him differently than if the same man were driving a Hyundai and wearing dirty jeans and a baseball cap.

Work also is a vehicle for a man to have an impact on his world. Deep down, both men and women want to know that their lives have made a difference. Men most often seek to make that difference through their careers. Work has to be more than an honest day's work for an honest day's wage. Work seems empty if it is not meaningful. Sir Oliver Wendell Holmes once said, "Nothing is so commonplace as to wish to be remarkable."

Bruce had a stable job as a computer technician. He was good at his work, but not the best or the brightest. He was but a small piece of the puzzle of a large corporation. He had never met the board of directors, the CEO, or the thousands of stockholders who owned it. He knew that at any time, he was expendable. Someone else could step in and fill his small shoes.

The technology that Bruce worked on every day was hard to describe to others. Neither his friends nor his wife actually understood what he did at the office. They simply knew that Bruce worked with computers. After a while, he had given up trying to explain it to them. His life consisted of dutifully dragging himself out of bed every morning, enduring the grueling commute and putting his time in at work. At 5:30 each afternoon, he retraced his steps and crept through rush hour traffic. He walked through the door every evening about 6:30, kissed his wife and kids, ate meat loaf, watched a couple hours of TV and then prepared for the next day's drudgery.

Rarely would Bruce allow himself to express the doubts that plagued him. Only during an occasional sleepless night could he be honest with his questions. "There has to be more to life than this! What I do does not even matter. I still have twenty more years until retirement. Some guys love their work. Why can't I have a job like that?" The pressures of bills, braces, car repairs and vacations kept Bruce's nose to the grindstone. But his wife could sense his discontentment. Not having the answer to his problem, she tried to ignore his doubts.

The heart of Bruce's despair was that he felt insignificant.

He spent thousands of hours in a building where people did not care about him or value what he individually contributed. For Bruce to be satisfied at work, he needed to believe his contribution really mattered.

The Frustration of His Work

Work is the ultimate enigma for a man. Even if he wins the lottery and never has to do a day's work in his life, he still needs work to survive. Men who retire, without replacing their paid jobs with other meaningful work, invariably feel depressed and useless. Work is both a blessing and a curse.

The book of Ecclesiastes sheds light on the dilemma of work. Solomon tells the story of his search for meaning through his activities. As a powerful king, Solomon had the freedom to pursue many aspects of work: wealth, power, pleasure and making the world a better place. Solomon attained them all, and he had this to say: "Vanity of vanities! All is vanity!"

As for wealth, Solomon lamented that appetites are never satisfied. No matter how much a man has, he will always want more. Solomon also notes that a rich man dies with nothing. He will leave all he has worked for to some man who does not deserve it. The richest men in the world die empty in the middle of their wealth.

Solomon also experienced the futility of power. During his time, he was the most powerful man alive. He despised his power in the end, acknowledging that people would inevitably criticize what he did with his influence. Imagine being the president of the United States. No matter how good a job you do, a large segment of the population will resent you and disagree with you. You could not open a newspaper or turn on the television without seeing someone's critical opinion or insulting parody. Surely "this too is meaningless and chasing after the wind" (Ecclesiastes 4:16, NIV).

Many men work in order to earn pleasure. They save until they can afford their coveted vacation or their dream of retirement. They want to enjoy life and have fun. In fact, many push through the week, driven by the hope of fun on the weekend. Their life is an endless cycle of work so they can experience pleasure. Solomon admits that there is a place for pleasure. He says it is good to enjoy the fruits of your work and the blessings of God. But living for pleasure is as empty as striving after the wind (Ecclesiastes 2, NIV).

Some men invest in their work because they believe in what they do. They trust that they can make the world a better place. They seek wisdom to solve the world's problems, hoping to help their fellow man. They may even be striving to win God's approval by their hard work for humanity. Solomon knew something about that, too. He discovered that thousands before him had discovered every thought of his. He also realized that many of the world's problems could never be solved by his wisdom or good intentions. "What is twisted cannot be straightened; what is lacking cannot be counted. . . . This, too, is a chasing after the wind. For with much wisdom comes much sorrow; the more knowledge, the more grief" (Ecclesiastes 1:15, 17, 18, NIV).

No wonder Solomon said, "So I hated life, because the work that is done under the sun was grievous to me"

(Ecclesiastes 2:17, NIV). (Solomon's wife obviously had the same problems with her husband that you have with yours!) After all of his soul-searching and griping about work, Solomon concluded that work is hard and ultimately feels empty.

You must take to heart the conflict that your husband likely feels regarding his work. Ultimately, he spends years of his life investing in a job or career that will bring little lasting fulfillment. His work will be tedious, discouraging and futile at times. God's curse to Adam in Genesis 3 guarantees such struggles. However, work is a God-ordained activity that is part of the experience of manhood. Having the right perspective of work will be immeasurably helpful as you encourage him through decades of failures, conflicts, decisions and setbacks.

So What Can I Do?

"Without a vision, the people will perish" (Proverbs 29:18, NASV). "As a man thinks within himself, so is he" (Proverbs 23:7, NASV). These verses are frequently used to support the positive-thinking preaching of motivational gurus like Robert Schuller, Tony Robbins, Earl Nightingale, Jack Canfield and Stephen Covey. These authors and speakers have each made millions of dollars. Do you know why? Because we love hearing that our dreams can come true. We are yearning for someone to tell us that it is okay to believe in our dreams. People who kill our passion and limit our vision surround us.

This is why a wife's response to her husband's dream is

critical to the health of their marriage. He can either see her as his greatest supporter or as a colossal party pooper.

It is natural for a wife to feel threatened by her husband's dream. She wants to be the center of his attention. A passion for anything else will surely compete with his affection for her. What a fatal mistake this becomes! As she discourages and even thwarts his dream, she slowly becomes his adversary. She is the one, in his mind, who has prevented him from reaching his true potential. "If it were not for her, I could have . . ." Many husbands harbor deep resentment toward their wives for secretly sabotaging their dreams.

On the other hand, the woman who supports and molds her husband's dreams becomes his intimate ally, his indispensable partner. Every idea he has, each success and each failure, he wants to share with her. Men are so thirsty for someone to believe in them that they willingly lap up expensive encouragement from strangers speaking to thousands. These performers say little more than this: "Dust off your dreams. You can live them. Do not give up!"

What do you suppose would happen if you started nurturing your husband's dream? How would you like to have his attention riveted on you, longing for your next date together? Here are some ways you can become part of your husband's dream.

Help Him Discover His Dream

In a story passed down for generations, Michelangelo was once asked how he knew what to carve when he crafted sculptures. His response was that God had created each stone to be a work of art. His job was to unlock the beautiful image that lay within the stone. According to Michelangelo, it was not his job to create. As a great artist, he carefully uncovered the unique masterpiece that God had placed in each rock.

What a wonderful metaphor for wives. It is not up to a woman to create a great man out of her husband. It is her calling to skillfully uncover the passions and abilities that God has given her spouse. She must be careful not to project her own wishes, desires and dreams onto him. A strong man is one who is fulfilling his own calling, not his wife's. For some women, this is a significant obstacle. Perhaps part of a wife's "dream" is to be married to a professional, or to never have to worry about finances. If her husband's passion is to be a high-school football coach, she has to yield her own desires in order to support his dream.

Do you have an idea of what your husband's dreams are? If you are like most women, you have only a vague idea. In fact, your husband may not even know where his passions lie. This endeavor is not something that happens overnight or even over a year. As your husband matures, his dream will evolve. Truly understanding his abilities, longings and passions is a quest that is accomplished over years of talking, listening, sharing and learning. Finding his dream may be a bit like digging in the ancient ruins of an archeological site. It will take patience, gentleness, determination and, perhaps, some nifty tools.

First, a man must be convinced that the environment is a safe one. He has probably been laughed at and discouraged so many times in his life that he is hesitant to share his dreams with anyone. If he has any doubt that his wife will be sensitive and loving, he is unlikely to risk vulnerability. Whatever he says, she must first listen intently and uncritically to convince him that she will not be another dream smasher.

A wife skillfully draws out her husband's dreams through thoughtful questions, listening and observations.

Start digging

A question can mean many different things. Questions can be critical, pressing or loaded—all of which shovel more dirt onto the pile rather than discovering what lies beneath.

- "You don't want to own your own business, do you?"
- "Do you think you are smart enough to get that degree?"
- "Where did you get that idea?"

These are all the wrong kinds of questions to ask. Skillful questions are sensitive and communicate, "I am interested in you. I want to understand who you really are." Here are a few examples of such questions:

- "What did you want to be when you were growing up? What did you like about the idea of being that? What do you think about that dream now?"
- "What do you think are your spiritual gifts? What special talents has God given you?"
- "If you could have any job in the world, what would it be? Why that particular job?"
- "What are some things that you really enjoy doing in your free time?"
- "What do you like about the job you have now?"

All of these questions are saying, "Dream away! I want to dream with you. I cannot really know you unless I know your dreams."

Listening

Have you ever talked with someone who asked good questions, but never really listened for the answer? In their eyes, you could tell they were thinking of their next question or mentally searching for a way to challenge what you just said. Listening is the hardest easy thing to do in the world. Some people pay $100 an hour or more, just to have an expert listener hear them. They do not want advice or counsel, they just want someone to really listen.

Even your most skillful questions will fall flat if you do not follow them up with really listening. As much as you are tempted, resist shooting down his ideas or dreams. Even if you already know what he will say, listen to learn through his voice tone, facial expressions or even through his silence.

Give him encouragement as he talks by nodding, touching his hand or shoulder and looking into his eyes. When you talk, make supportive comments like, "I never knew that about you." "I could see you being great at that." "You're right. You do have the gift of administration." With each moment that you truly listen, you are building a solid bridge in your marriage.

Observation

You can learn a lot about your husband by watching him. What does he get excited about? What does he look forward to? What does he dread doing? What kinds of people respond to him? How does he interact in a group? What makes him feel comfortable around others? Study him and learn.

It did not take me long to notice that my husband is a natural around kids. Whenever he's with children, Mike immediately creates the wildest games and uses the most entertaining voices. All of my nephews and nieces flock around him, waiting to be tossed into the air, wrestled to the ground or simply held. Mike is also wonderful with the elderly. He loves listening to their stories and he remembers every detail. These observations are clues that help me understand the unique dreams and talents that God has given to my husband.

For some men, finding their dream seems like a dead-end road. They cannot articulate what they enjoy or look forward to. To them, no job seems just right. In this case, investing in career testing at a local church or counseling center can be very helpful. Discovering his gifts, interests and abilities encourages a man to dream and to believe that God can use him in a special way.

Refining His Dream

So your husband's dream is to play professional basketball. He stands five feet six inches, thirty-eight years old, and barely manages to keep up with his church buddies when they play for fun. How are you going to believe in that dream?

This is the reality that some women face. Their husbands' dreams are simply unrealistic. Perhaps he wants to put the family in financial straits, while pursuing some risky fantasy of becoming a millionaire. Maybe his dream, at least to his wife, seems to be ungodly. Or maybe his dream changes every month. Now the waters are murky. How does a wife facilitate her husband's dreams without encouraging false or destructive hopes?

The key is to understand what is behind your husband's dream. Rarely is a man's dream simply to accomplish one feat, like climbing Mount Everest. A dream represents something about who a man is or wants to become.

Tom always dreamed of making lots of money. He did not know how he would make it, but he knew that in order to think of himself as successful, his ship must someday come in. He was obsessed with the trappings of wealth. Stuck in a dead-end job as a middle manager, Tom doubted that he would ever succeed. His wife, Sharon, could sense Tom's defeated attitude. She could never get behind Tom's dream. She knew that pursuing wealth would lead nowhere.

Sharon's discouragement and resistance were obvious to Tom. She rolled her eyes when he talked about investments. She chuckled when he asked for *Forbes* and *Money* magazines for Christmas. Although she came off as sarcastic and unsupportive, Sharon's real feelings were frustration, fear and sadness. She had difficulty respecting and loving Tom when his priorities were so out of place. Making money was the only thing he seemed to get truly excited about. He was willing to miss anniversaries, piano recitals and bedtime stories chasing down his dream. It was not fair to her or to the kids.

Although Sharon's frustrations were understandable and perhaps justified, she could channel her energy much more productively. Instead of resisting Tom's dream, Sharon could help Tom refine it. She could start with helpful (but not nagging) questions. Why was money so important to him?

What did he like about the wealthy people he knew? When did he first become aware of this dream? Was he willing to give up everything else to be rich? Could he imagine himself happy without great wealth? If so, how?

Most likely, deep emotions are rooted in Tom's dream. Perhaps he equates wealth with significance. If this were the case, could Sharon help him find other ways to be significant? What is really behind his dream? What does he need to feel important and fulfilled?

It may take years. However, after patient encouragement and support, Tom might realize that he really wants to be respected by others. He could begin to earn their respect through his integrity and character. Now his refined dream is to live with integrity, so that people see him as different from others. This is a dream that Sharon can support wholeheartedly. It is also a passion that Tom can achieve no matter where he works.

Refining your husband's dream means understanding what he is longing to express about himself. Go beyond what he wants to do. Who does he want to be?

Linking the Dream with a Job

Perhaps one of the greatest frustrations for a man is working hour after hour in a job that has nothing to do with his passion. Every day, he feels as if he is wasting precious time and energy. As the clock ticks to middle age, he begins to fear that he may never achieve his dream. His life is so filled with going through the motions that he has forgotten how to live. He cannot remember what it felt like to be passionate or excited. Work and all of the people that keep him trapped in the day-to-day grind become the enemy of his passion. This dynamic is often what underlies the phenomena known as "mid-life crisis." It is, therefore, vital that a man have a sense of his dream and find a way to incorporate it into his daily life.

There are two keys to linking your husband's dream to reality. First of all, many dreams can be accomplished through an imperfect job. There is a big difference between finding "the perfect job" and finding a job through which a dream can be lived.

Many men flit from job to job seeking that perfect fit. Work is imperfect. The curse in Genesis 3:17–19 promises that it will always be flawed. For many, giving up the vision of the effortless, stress-free job is half the battle. It is impossible to appreciate a good situation when one's focus is on the illusion of perfection.

In many men's eyes, what job could be more perfect than playing professional sports? Earn a six- or seven-figure salary for playing a game you love a few months a year. Become rich and famous. Now, that's the life! I have a friend whose husband lives this "perfect" dream. He lives one injury away from no income. He sits on the sidelines waiting for the coach to give him the chance to prove what he can do. He endures the jeering and criticism from the media when he makes a mistake. He faces the pressure to use steroids to keep up with his competitors who do. He trains endlessly to avoid the inevitable decline of his strength and looming retirement in his mid-thirties. What will he do then?

When a man accepts that he will experience disappointment, frustration and setbacks in any career, he becomes free to pour himself into his work. Otherwise, he reserves his passion and energy for the "perfect" opportunity that may be just around the corner. Of course, some jobs are more desirable than others. Ideally, as a man ages, he should be working closer to a good fit. However, no job will be free of stress or conflict.

Even if he does not love where he works, a man can work at what he loves. Practically any job can become a vehicle to work toward aspects of a man's dream. Even if he does not get the raise, the promotion or the admiration of his colleagues, he can be considerate, honest, hardworking and content. For example, every task that a man faces is a chance to achieve the dream of following Christ—of displaying his character in all circumstances. How better to define victory or success? However, it is a dream that is easily overlooked. When was the last time you encouraged your husband for his character at work? You will likely be the only one in his life who will highlight the importance of such a dream.

The second key to linking dreams with reality is understanding that not all dreams will be fulfilled through the wage-earning job. There are many ways for a man to accomplish his dreams outside of his nine-to-five routine.

Rick had always dreamed of owning a camp for disabled children. With three kids of his own, a mortgage, bills and credit card debt, Rick was locked into his job as an accountant. His dream, realistically, could not even be approached, at least for many years. So what should his wife do? Forget that

Rick even had a dream, since it would have to remain unfulfilled?

Rick's dream could remain alive and well even while maintaining his job as an accountant. He may not be able to own a camp, but he could certainly volunteer at one. Rick could also be involved in fund-raising for causes like Special Olympics or research on spina bifida.

Most of the disciples of the early church maintained their mundane jobs while pursuing their passion to follow Christ and spread the gospel. Paul was a tentmaker, Luke was a doctor and Mark a fisherman. In fact, Jesus was a carpenter. Their jobs provided them contact with people, respect in the community and provision for their ministry.

Men can also pursue their dreams through leisure. My husband loves adventure. A part of him would love to be a missionary pilot, flying down a river to rescue people out of the jungle. At eighteen, he had his pilot's license and his scuba license. Before we met, he was a Marine who jumped out of airplanes on a regular basis. Now he is a banker with a wife and two kids. Needless to say, his passion for adventure has suffered.

When we first married, I tried to discourage the adventurer in him. Terrified of being widowed, I hated his daring hobbies. When our children were born, I insisted that he take no unnecessary risks. Then I realized that a part of him was dying. Together, we have found some ways for him to experience relatively safe adventures in the middle of his workaday life. For example, we try to incorporate adventure (white-water rafting, skiing, hang gliding) whenever we take vacations.

Practical Issues on the Job

As stressful as a husband's job may be, it is almost as frustrating for his wife. She watches him struggle, worry and blunder. All she can do, it seems, is watch. She cannot rescue him from stress, frustration or failure. She cannot force him to leave work at the office. She cannot convince him that his work is meaningful. She cannot make him go to work when he gives up.

As helpless as she feels, a wife's involvement in her husband's work does have an impact. As in any other aspect of marriage, her influence can either be a positive force or a negative one.

Remember, It Is His Work

"I care about my husband's work. I ask him about it all the time, but he never takes my advice. In fact, he never wants to talk about work." As damaging as it is for a wife to undervalue her husband's work, it is equally destructive for her to take personal responsibility for his job.

As their husbands come home and vent about frustrations at work, some wives have a special knack at pointing out what he did wrong and how he can fix it.

Mike recently caught me playing the "expert" at his job. I was confidently giving him tips on making sales calls. He reminded me of the fact that I break out in hives whenever I have to place an unpleasant telephone call. "You have no idea what I do at work," he said firmly. He was right. He needed me to listen. He definitely did not need me to tell him how I could do his job better than he could!

This is a tempting trap for a woman to fall into. She relies on his income as much as he does. However, she feels like a helpless cheerleader on the sideline. He handles work so differently than she would. What if he "drops the ball?" What her worry and advice really tell him is, "I don't trust you. We would be better off if I were the one earning the paycheck."

He will make mistakes. However, they are his mistakes to make. Be his advocate, his friend, his encourager and his sounding board. But don't be his boss or his critic. In fact, be careful about being his advisor. Opinions and perspectives can be helpful, but advice from a wife can be threatening to some husbands. Rather than coaching him through his job, encourage your husband to find a mentor who knows about his job and the unique pressures of being a man.

When Your Husband Won't Work

Megan had a great job as an administrative assistant to an executive. She earned a significant salary with benefits and paid vacation time. Her husband, Bryan, earned less than she did. He never really liked work. He tried carpentry, plumbing, trucking and even computers. About a year into each job, he gave up, frustrated by the long hours and low pay. Bryan was not getting any younger. Each time he switched professions, he started back at the beginning. Only now, Bryan's bosses were younger than he.

Megan and Bryan had two children within eighteen months.

After brief maternity leaves, Megan returned to work and put the children in day care. The family simply could not afford to have her quit work. Not long after their second child was born, Bryan again quit his job. After months of searching and interviewing, Bryan decided that it would be cheaper for him to stay home with the kids than work.

As the children grew and entered school, Bryan still resisted finding a job. Now thirty-five, with no college degree and no marketable skills, Bryan felt useless. He couldn't imagine working at a gas station while Megan's career soared. Seeking work would mean facing the ultimate humiliation.

More and more couples today are finding themselves like Bryan and Megan. With very few exceptions, these marriages end in desperate straits. Men avoid work for a variety of reasons. Usually, however, their reasons revolve around fear of failure. Their competent, consistent and marketable wives flourish on the job while they flounder in failure.

In some cases, a man simply cannot work. He may be physically unable to work due to a legitimate disability. Other times, a couple decides that the husband will temporarily care for their children while she works. The husband then assumes all of the household tasks and domestic responsibilities. In my experience as a psychologist, this arrangement is rarely successful long-term. Although it is not advisable, in this scenario both the man and the women are making significant contributions to the family. This is different from a man who will not work and refuses to assume meaningful responsibilities.

It is imperative that a woman not take over for a man who opts out of work. Her motives may be innocent enough in the beginning. However, she will one day regret giving him the "get out of work free" card. In his letter to the church at Thessalonians, Paul addressed men who did not provide for their families:

For even when we were with you, we gave you this rule: "If a man will not work, he shall not eat." We hear that some among you are idle. They are not busy; they are busybodies. Such people we command and urge in the Lord Jesus Christ to settle down and earn the bread they eat. . . . If anyone does not obey our instructions in this letter, take special note of him. Do not associate with him, in order that he may feel ashamed. Yet do not regard him as an enemy, but warn him as a brother.

II Thessalonians 3:10–15, NIV

So, what should a wife, like Megan, do when her husband will not work? First, she should make an effort to encourage her husband vocationally. Part of this may be downplaying her own career success. For example, she can resist highlighting how much more money or prestige her job brings compared to his. She can also praise his work, regardless of the amount of income it brings.

A wife in this situation may also need to stop enabling her husband's laziness. Although she needs to continue to work to feed herself and her children, she forces her husband to face his lack of contribution to the family. For example, she may refuse to do any household task for her husband (doing his laundry, cooking his meals). The money that she earns, in this case, should also not pay for his expenses (for example, his car or hobbies). These strategies are not meant to be either manipulative or vindictive. A wife would respond this way only to avoid enabling her husband's fears, avoidance and idleness. Her interventions are a form of tough love. She is essentially telling him, "God has called you to be more than this. I will not be partner to your attempts to avoid responsibility. I cannot make you responsible, but I can refuse to encourage irresponsibility."

When Your Husband Won't Stop Working

Mary never worried about Gerald having an affair. She knew that he loved her and that other women did not tempt him. Nevertheless, Mary still felt like a rejected wife. Night after night, she sat home waiting for him to come home for dinner. She looked forward to weekends when she might spend time with him. But Gerald was consistent. He was always working. Even on vacation, his mind was preoccupied with ideas, problems and plans for his company. Mary felt as if her husband had a mistress—his job.

Workaholic is a word that became popular around 1980. Yes, men can become addicted to their jobs. Clearly it is not their work to which they are addicted—it is the excitement, the risk, the drive for success or the fear of failure. What is a wife to do with her driven husband?

As any addiction, the drive to work is very hard to break. Pleading, screaming, crying and threatening will all likely fall on deaf ears. In fact, nagging may actually have the opposite effect and may encourage him to spend even more time at work. Why would a neglectful husband rush home if he expects to be read the riot act?

Unfortunately, there is no quick fix for a husband who is married to his job. However, a few things may make a difference over time:

1. *Love the man, not his success.* Men (and women) become addicted to performance when they believe that they must constantly earn the approval or esteem of others. A workaholic has often has learned, at a very young age, that hard work and achievement can compensate for shortcomings. This is a lesson that is routinely reinforced. Everyone cheers for a winner. It is easy for parents and friends to pay more attention to someone when they are excelling.

   The steady love of a wife who stays consistent through success and failure can be a powerful antidote to performance addiction. "You don't have to perform for me. Your success or failure can never change my love for you. When you succeed I am happy for you, but it will never alter how much I value you." What a powerful message to live daily in marriage!

2. *Support his dream, not his drive.* Workaholics often live for their drive rather than for their dream. A dream is defined by passion and enthusiasm for something. A drive is characterized by compulsion. Many men give up their dreams in order to satisfy their drive. Unlike

dreams, drives can never be fulfilled. When a man dreams, he is moving toward something—a goal, a purpose, a worthy personality characteristic, a calling. When a man is driven, he is moving away from something he fears—failure, rejection and emptiness. Dreams move a person closer to their uniqueness. Drives move them further into the recesses of their defensiveness.

Darin was driven to be the best. He had to prove to his parents and everyone else that he was superior to all of his colleagues. When everyone cleared the office at six, he stayed until nine. Naturally, he climbed the ladder of success rapidly. After years of eating, sleeping and drinking his work, Darin had neglected his dreams. He had no hobbies, little time for people and no leisure. To his wife, Susan, Darin had become a working machine. Their marriage revolved around his work. He did not know how to talk about anything else. As a dutiful husband, he listened to Susan drone on about her day, but with little interest. Only a distant memory was the passion they had shared while dating, when they had talked about ideas, served in a church and dreamed of the future.

A man's wife may be the only person who knows him well enough to differentiate between his dream and his drive. She is likely the only one who can prompt him to think about why he works so many hours. Through her influence, she can assuage his fear and ignite his passion. A drive is always an enemy to a dream. A wife will invariably support one or the other. However, even the perfect wife can only do so much to encourage her husband to work through his insecurity. Ultimately, this is something that he must choose to confront.

3. *Encourage him to reflect on his life.* There are times when people naturally sit back and take stock of their lives. For many, milestones such as birthdays or holidays are the time to do so. Others think about their lives while on vacation or even when they are sick.

   Take advantage of these times when your husband is reevaluating. Help him ask the right questions. Through your thoughtful comments and prompts, ask him what he might regret years from now. Encourage him to think about why work has such a hold on him. Remind him of how important he is to you and his children.

A husband is unlikely to drop his obsession with work just because his wife suggests it. This is a change that he must make as he matures. She can only facilitate that process by listening and encouraging his personal growth. This means that she will also have to be patient and prayerful. This is a change that she cannot force.

But I Have Dreams, Too!

Many women have spent years, even decades, listening to and nurturing their husband's dreams. Over the years, they have grown resentful as they look back to see their own dreams faded. "I earned a college degree in teaching and never even used it," one woman lamented. "I spent my adult life following my husband from city to city as his career demanded. What about my dreams?"

Does a wife have to sacrifice her passions in order to support her husband's dream? It is hard enough tackling one person's goals. How can a couple possibly work toward both of their dreams?

The ideal is always for a husband and wife to support each other's dreams. At different points in life, one may take precedence. However, if one person stops dreaming, this is cause for concern. If after thirty years of marriage, a husband has not achieved his dream, he will likely blame his wife. The same is true of a wife. After the children are grown and her life feels empty, her husband will easily become the culprit of talents wasted and dreams in the dust. Keep the dreams alive!

My husband and I meet regularly for planning sessions that help keep us mindful of each other's dreams. About once or twice a year, we get away for the weekend and talk. We share the goals that we each have for the next year and next five years. We talk about where we are personally and in our marriage. As we share, we learn about the dreams, hopes and fears that we rarely discuss in everyday life.

Although each husband and wife will have individual goals, it is also important to have some dreams that you share. Writing a family mission statement can be a starting point. Another way to dream together is to compile a list of 100 things that you would like to do together in your lifetime. Brainstorm. Some may be simple (trying Rollerblading), missions-oriented (buying Christmas dinner for a family in need), or even outrageous (traveling to Japan). Nothing creates a feeling of companionship like sharing and working toward the same dreams.

Hold fast to dreams
For if dreams die
Life is a broken-winged bird
That cannot fly.
  (Langston Hughes, *Dreams*)

Does your marriage feel like a broken-winged bird? Is passion for life only a distant memory? Dust off those dreams. Encourage your husband to dream with you. Pray that God will renew the passion for life, marriage, ministry and your family.

The wise woman builds her house, but with her own hands the foolish one tears hers down.

Proverbs 14:1, NIV

Questions for Discussion and Reflection

1. Why is work such an important aspect of your husband's life? How does his work affect your marriage? How does your marriage affect his work?

2. Read Genesis 3:17–19 and Ecclesiastes 1:17–18; 2:10–11, 22–23; 6:7 and 8:17. Why will work always be frustrating?

3. What do you know about your husband's dreams? To what extent does his life reflect his dreams? What are your dreams? To what extent does your life reflect your dreams? How do your dreams affect your husband's dreams and vice versa?

4. What are some practical ways you can encourage your husband's dreams? How can you share your dreams with him? How can you dream together?

5. What is your husband's greatest challenge related to his work? How can you help him with this challenge?

Eleven

No More
"Headaches"

omen are not opposed to the idea of great sex. A trip to the local grocery market proves this. Blaring from their racks in the checkout line are half a dozen magazines boasting tantalizing articles like "Ten Sex Secrets You Must Know," "The Fifteen Secrets of Sexy Wives," "Is Your Lover Happy in Bed?" and "Keeping Your Man Coming Back For More." Such promises must sell or they would soon disappear from the shelves. Despite this fact, many wives have learned to dread sex or, at most, be neutral towards it. "Who needs sex? I'd be happy with a cup of tea and a good book," one client told me. Another lamented, "Just cuddling and hugging are enough to keep me satisfied. I wouldn't mind if we never had sex again."

Why the dichotomy? Do women want sex or don't they? Like so many other aspects of marriage, reality in the bedroom is often far below what most women once hoped to experience. After years of images from television, movies and romance novels, they expected sex to be wonderfully pleasurable and fulfilling. For some, it is. But for most, their marital sex lives have left much to be desired. Even when it is good, it seems to take too much time, energy and effort.

The luring promises the articles make symbolize the hope of many women that sex can somehow be more than the everyday reality of the marriage bed.

Causes of the Common "Headache" and Their Antidotes

"My wife will do anything to avoid sex. She is always too busy, too tired, too dressed up or too angry with me to be interested in intercourse. If all else fails, she has a headache!" Derrick complained. "I don't know where she expects me to get my needs met. Sex has become a great conflict for us."

Both husbands and wives in many marriages feel discouraged about their sexual relationship. A great sex life within marriage is very difficult to sustain because so many problems can interfere with sexual fulfillment. Literally hundreds of things can go wrong, leaving both partners frustrated and angry. Although the solution may not be as simple as the ones advertised at the grocery store, there is help available.

Emotional Problems

Some people make the mistake of characterizing sex as just a physical act. Of course, it involves the body, but sex is also very emotional. It requires relaxation, focus and letting go. Each of these are greatly affected by negative emotions like anxiety and fear.

I have recently begun speaking at couples' and women's retreats on the topic of sex. As I look around the room, I notice how people react just to the mention of the word "sex." Some turn many shades of red, others giggle nervously and some busily take notes in order to avoid making eye contact. There is no denying that sex evokes tremendous emotions. Those feelings may be pleasant, uncomfortable or even terrifying.

A person's reaction to sex is often directly related to one's view of sex. People learn about sex in different contexts. Some children are told by their parents that it is dirty and evil. Perhaps they were scolded as children for touching their genitals. Other people learn about sex through traumatic experiences or promiscuous adolescent behavior. Even in the absence of "teaching," silence on the topic is a powerful teacher. Only a fortunate few learned early that sex is a beautiful gift of God to be enjoyed within the safety of marriage.

There is a lot of talk today about self-image. However, most people are unaware of their "sexual self-image." We are all sexual creatures. We all have different feelings about that fact. While some people see themselves as highly sexual, other people deny everything sexual about themselves. Sexual self-esteem can be affected by a variety of factors, both big and small.

"I cannot have sex with the lights on. I feel so self-conscious about my body," Beth explained. Discontent with physical appearance is something that many women deal with. Exposure to slim, seductive models and movie stars only serves to highlight the flaws and imperfections of the average body: too skinny, too fat, too flabby, too flat, too busty, too pale, too wrinkly. Some research suggests that up to 85 percent of adult women are dissatisfied with their bodies. Certainly this affects a woman's sexual self-esteem. How can she feel beautiful and seductive when she compares so unfavorably to what she and her husband see in the world?

Deeper issues related to trauma have an even greater impact on sexual self-esteem. Vicky's childhood included a few episodes that left a lasting impression on her view of her sexuality. Although she never considered herself a victim of abuse, Vicky had a stepfather who often made inappropriate comments toward her. He regularly teased her about her sexual development and "playfully" pinched her chest and bottom during her adolescent years. Vicky felt very confused about her sexuality. She dealt with it by focusing on school and hobbies and avoided dating.

In her mid-twenties, she married Doug. The problems for Vicky and Doug began almost immediately. Vicky was anxious about sex. She felt dirty and uncomfortable any time Doug tried to look at her or touch her. The two had intercourse occasionally, and then, only to fulfill Doug's physical desires. When they did make love, Vicky was so anxious that her body was never ready for intercourse. Doug's penetration was painful for her, which made her dread sex even more.

Vicky and Doug's problems poignantly illustrate how a poor "sexual self-image" can snowball into a considerable conflict for a couple. In order to be a good lover, a person must be able to accept herself as a sexual person who is able to both give and receive love.

Over the years, you may have tried to undo the harmful messages you learned as a child. Even if you have succeeded in understanding the beauty and dignity of sex, your immediate emotional response may still be one of fear, insecurity or guilt. Emotional memories are extremely difficult to replace. Being touched may bring instant feelings of anxiety. Even negative sexual experiences within marriage can result in emotional "baggage" in the bedroom. Fear of failure, pain, rejection or humiliation are hurdles for many men and women within their sexual relationship.

The Antidote

Overcoming emotional hurdles in sex can be difficult. Feelings of insecurity can only be addressed within the safety of a committed relationship. A couple must work together to confront the challenges to enjoying the ultimate intimacy.

It can be difficult for many women to see themselves as sexual. Perhaps all their lives they have been told not to act or dress in a way that captures a man's attention. All of a sudden, they are supposed to be sensual with their husbands. Successfully making this transition is a tremendous challenge.

God created both men and women as sexual and said that it was "very good." What the world has done with sex is not good. Worldly attitudes, however, do not have to taint what God created to be a wonderful demonstration of love and intimacy in marriage.

The world may have tainted your view of your own sexuality. Allow God to restore it within your marriage. Work with him to redeem it. It is right to think sexually about your husband. It is wonderful to enjoy his touch and his passion for you. God created you to long for closeness. Whatever roadblocks you are up against, work through them. Seek counseling, read helpful literature, pray for healing—but do not give up.

Counseling is often necessary to address problems stemming back to painful experiences like abuse, promiscuity or abortions. These issues are deeply rooted and do not disappear without significant emotional and spiritual healing. Clifford and Joyce Penner's book *Restoring the Pleasure* is an excellent guide for couples who long to overcome emotional roadblocks to sexual fulfillment. A husband and wife who together seek healing may discover profound intimacy through the difficult journey that they share.

Poor Sexual Boundaries

The term "boundaries" has become a well-known pop-psychology concept over the past few years. Boundaries certainly apply to the sexual aspect of marriage. A popular understanding of sex has made its greatest mistake in reversing the boundaries of pure and intimate sex.

There are two sets of boundaries that are present in every sexual relationship. The first boundary is between the couple and the rest of the world. The second boundary is the amount of access the husband and wife have to each other.

In the world's view of sex, the first boundary is very open. Thoughts and images of other people, other places, sights and sounds are permitted and even encouraged. For example, many sex therapists suggest that couples watch pornography together to enhance their experience. The main problem with a weak boundary between the world and the couple is that it trivializes the purity of sex. Focusing on anything other than each other sexually is a form of adultery. Jesus says as much in Matthew 5:27–28.

Another way of weakening this boundary is a casual attitude towards sex. What happens between a husband and a wife should be kept sacred. Sexual jokes, sharing with friends, and the media's causal attitude towards sexuality all serve to tear down this boundary. It is extremely difficult in today's culture to protect the purity of your sexual relationship.

The second boundary, on the other hand, is often thick and rigid. Each person has his or her own feelings and fantasies, which they would rarely communicate to the other. He is thinking of the Playmate of the Month while she fantasizes about Tom Cruise. This may be sex, but it certainly is not the intimacy that God intended.

When this boundary becomes rigid, intimacy is impossible. Sexual closeness involves more than two naked bodies. It requires two naked souls. The two become one—not just in their bodies. They share thoughts, feelings, fears and experiences. Particularly for the women, this is an integral part of sexual intimacy. If it is missing, she will likely be quick to lose interest.

THE WORLD'S VIEW OF SEXUAL BOUNDARIES

Boundary #2

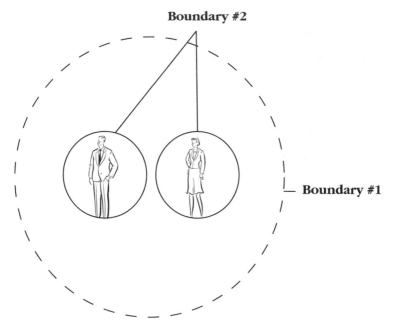

Boundary #1

Warren and Diane were very frustrated in their sexual relationship. They worked on fixing the problem for years before bringing their struggle up in counseling. As they discussed their sex life, it became obvious that the boundaries in their sexual relationship were all wrong.

Both Warren and Diane relied heavily on fantasy to get themselves excited about sex. Diane, in particular, was concerned about this. She felt guilty when she imagined scenes from movies or thought about being with other men during intimacy with her husband. She was outraged to learn that Warren occasionally used pornography. As they discussed this issue, they both felt as if their sexual relationship had been tainted. The reality of their monotonous sex life could not compete with the sensuality of their fantasy.

They were both rather embarrassed about what they thought about during sex with each other. Naturally, the communication in their sexual relationship suffered. They both worked individually to experience pleasure during sex without sharing more than physical space. Over time, their sexual relationship had become lifeless.

The Antidote

A healthy sexual relationship is characterized by the exact opposite of Warren's and Diane's pattern. Boundary number one must be very secure. No one should be allowed symbolically or physically within the sanctuary of their sexual relationship. Both the husband and wife must use great discretion in what they share with others, and what they allow from the world into their own minds. Their sexual relationship is something that they treasure and protect. It is as if the two of them share a secret that no one else in the world knows about.

Boundary number two, however, should be very diffuse. Both need to make a concerted effort to communicate their thoughts, feelings and experiences. They should each strive to know right where the other person is emotionally, spiritually and physically.

A Biblical View of Sexual Boundaries

Boundary #2

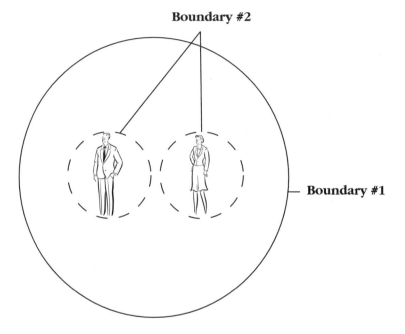

— **Boundary #1**

Appropriately maintaining both boundaries presents significant challenges. For the first boundary, many forces push their way into the marriage. Images, movies, advice and gossip can all threaten to weaken the wall of safety around the couple. A couple must always be on guard to maintain the "fence" around their sexual purity.

One of the greatest barriers to keeping the boundary between the couple open is fear during sex. Fears of intimacy, failure, touch, pain or traumatic memories all make a husband or wife dread being fully present during intimacy. It feels safer to distance themselves from the sensations, smells and sounds. Thinking about anything else but the act becomes a way of coping with fears related to intimacy. However, this defense comes with the price of compromising the intensity of the couple's physical and emotional oneness. These fears must be resolved in order for a couple to communicate with each other both during sex and about sex.

For many women, their friends know more about their sex lives than their husbands do. Talking together about sex is very difficult for both husbands and wives. It requires overcoming anxiety, social norms, fears and embarrassment. A couple simply cannot navigate through all of the obstacles of sexuality without very open, loving communication.

Communication Exercise:

This exercise will facilitate communication between you and your husband concerning your sexual relationship. Write your responses individually and then share them with each other during a solid block of uninterrupted time. (This may take more than one conversation.)

What, when and from whom did you learn about sex?

What were your parents' attitudes toward sex when you were growing up? How did they respond to your questions about sex?

Have you had any traumatic sexual experiences as a child? Adolescent? Adult?

In your marriage, how often do you initiate sexual activity? How often does your spouse initiate sexual activity? How do you wish this might be different?

Describe the typical process of initiation of sexual intercourse for you and your spouse. (Who does what and how does the other respond?)

What does or what would help the two of you to connect (bring your worlds together)?

What tends to get you sexually aroused? What kind of touching is most pleasurable for you? Do you like to be talked to during sexual activity?

What inhibitions get in the way of the two of you freely enjoying the process of being together? What sexual activities cause conflict between the two of you?

What percentage of the time is lovemaking a good experience for you? For your spouse?

How often are you and your spouse sexually intimate? How frequently do you desire sexual intimacy? How frequently does your spouse?

What do you usually do and feel after intercourse? What do you sense from your spouse? How might you be more sensitive to each other's needs for affirmation?

Adapted with permission from *Restoring the Pleasure* by Clifford and Joyce Penner.

As Goes the Marriage, So Goes Sex

I have never been much of a cook. With three sisters and a mother who all cook and bake masterfully, I had no reason to learn how. Now that I am a wife and mother, I have reluctantly accepted my role as the family chef. Recently, I attempted to bake a homemade cake for a dinner party. I measured all of the ingredients carefully, preheated the oven and baked my cake at the exact temperature the recipe called for.

When the timer went off, I anxiously opened the oven to see a lopsided brown lump waiting for me. Since our company was arriving shortly, I did not have time to whip up a substitute dessert. I grabbed the frosting and tried to spread it thickly so it would cover up the deformed cake. To my chagrin, the frosting proved useless. It simply took on the lumpy and lopsided form of the cake. I covered my mistake by cleverly announcing to our friends that three-year-old Michael had helped me make dessert!

Sex is truly the icing on the cake. It will always take on the form of the relationship, even for couples who try to use it to cover up other problems or to think of it as a separate issue. Many couples come to counseling complaining of problems sexually. Almost invariably, their sexual dynamics are a perfect illustration of what is happening throughout their entire relationship. This is why working on the sexual relationship alone will be inadequate to solve the underlying problems in the marriage.

A fulfilling, exciting sexual relationship is impossible, over time, if two people have significant conflict. When marital conflict is not resolved, it never disappears but multiplies with time. Seething hostility, repressed anger and bitterness will all eventually manifest as a "headache." Particularly for women, anger destroys any thought of physical or emotional vulnerability.

Just like emotional intimacy in marriage, sexual intimacy works on trust and communication. If each person's vulnerabilities are protected and their needs are met, they will become more and more intimate sexually. If they feel insecure, exploited or unsafe, their physical intimacy will become unsatisfying, superficial and infrequent. The good news is that every day presents an opportunity to change the momentum of a failing emotional or sexual relationship.

Since in many marriages the husband initiates more often, for this illustration, we will assume he is initiating. However, similar dynamics occur when the roles are reversed. Whenever a husband initiates sexually, he is taking a risk. He can only wait for her response, which will be either affirming or rejecting.

DYNAMICS OF SEXUAL INTIMACY

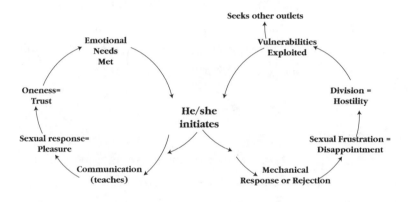

Each sexual initiation can lead to a path of frustration and isolation. A wife can flat-out reject her husband's advance. "In your dreams!" or "No thank you. I'm not interested," can do the trick. Equally effective are her nonverbal cues like walking away, tensing her body or a condescending look. Surprisingly, a mechanical sexual response has the same effect. She can go through the motions with only one thought, "Just get it over with!" Her husband may have his physical needs met, but emotionally, he is no closer to her.

After outright rejection or a frigid response, either or both the husband and the wife are left feeling frustrating and disappointed. He feels humiliated and inadequate. She may feel cheapened, like a sexual object. Over time, this gift of God that was meant to bring oneness has led to hostility and resentment between husband and wife. Neither feels safe sexually or emotionally. Future sexual encounters are either avoided or approached with great anxiety.

When a couple has gained negative momentum in their sexual relationship, other outlets will be used for sexual and emotional intimacy. Men and women have both physical and emotional drives that are intended to be met within their marriage. When they are not, both the husband and wife are vulnerable to influences outside of their relationship.

The Antidote

Fortunately, each sexual encounter is also an opportunity to build the sexual momentum in a positive direction. The best thing a wife can do when her husband initiates is to lovingly communicate (verbally and nonverbally) what is going on with her. She may respond by interacting sexually with him. However, she may also say something like, "My mind is on what I have to do tomorrow. Let me finish writing this down and then I can focus on being with you." Or, "Could we talk for a little bit first? That would help me feel closer to you." Or even, "I am exhausted right now. I really want to be with you, but now is a really bad time. Let's set up a date tomorrow morning to be together."

All of these responses help promote intimacy. They are affirming and also help communicate how a wife's sexual needs can be better met. It is especially important for a wife to communicate what she needs in order to respond sexually and emotionally to her husband's advances. She does this while also being mindful of his needs. Eventually, responding in a loving and honest way will lead to a sexual response that is emotionally pleasing to both people. The experience will promote trust and a sense of oneness sexually and emotionally. This is the ultimate fulfillment of God's design for sex. It is a wonderful expression of commitment and oneness that cements a couple's love.

Although responding lovingly to your husband's sexual advances will not likely save a struggling marriage, it can be an important symbolic step. Notice the similarities between the cycles of emotional intimacy described in chapter five and the cycle of physical intimacy in this chapter. Making an effort to work past your anger and defenses sexually can be a meaningful part of making the same effort towards emotional intimacy in your marriage.

The Temptation of Sexual Outlets

Men often gravitate towards fantasy or pornography as sexual outlets. The power of these temptations for many men cannot be overstated. Everywhere they go, it seems that sex is calling for them—billboards, magazines, radio, movies, television and the Internet. Proverbs 7:11–12 describes the harlot: "She is loud and defiant, her feet never stay at home; now in the street, now in the squares, at every corner she lurks (NIV)." This temptation may be especially difficult for men who travel. They are constantly bombarded in the area where they may feel the weakest. When their wives withhold sexually, husbands may justify dabbling in pornography or fantasy.

Men may also be emotionally attracted to other women when their marriages are failing. His attractive coworker shares ideas with him, spends time listening to his struggles and encourages his dreams. She does not know his faults and does not perceive him as a failure as his wife does. He is attractive and competent in her eyes. Why not go for it?

As women, we never get caught up in other sexual outlets. Right! Although the thought of a *Playgirl* or male stripper may not be a temptation for all women, she is also vulnerable to seeking satisfaction outside of her marriage. Most women relate to the idea of finding a hero. If her husband will not be her hero, she finds someone who will be.

Common outlets for women are romance novels and soap operas. These serve the same purpose as does pornography for men. Both promote a fantasy that make reality seem dreadfully dull and unsatisfying. Where in the world is a man named Sebastian who is gorgeous, strong, sensitive, rich and knows exactly what to say to make your heart melt and your toes curl? Such a creature does not exist. He is as unrealistic as a brilliant, logical female with flawless skin and perfect measurements.

I realized just what an effect this had on me when Mike and I rented the movie *The Bridges of Madison County.* I thought it was a very romantic flick. Then Mike reminded me that we were watching glorified adultery. The female character was not happy in her boring marriage and was swept off her feet by an adventurous hero. I had to be honest and admit this was a terrible fantasy for me to foster. What will I do when my marriage gets boring? The smut that is sold to women may not seem as distasteful as what they sell to our husbands, but it is just as destructive.

Women are also emotionally vulnerable to affairs when intimacy in their marriage fails. Over time, she feels like an awful combination of her husband's mother and his maid. Whatever sexual feelings she ever had disappeared years ago. Then one day, a dashing man compliments her. He makes her feel beautiful, smart and seductive. He looks into her eyes with a passion that her husband lost not long after their honeymoon. Why not? She deserves to be loved, doesn't she?

The Antidote

Marriage is difficult. Fostering a sexual relationship that is fulfilling over years is hard work. It means tears, fights, communication, risk, sacrifice and enduring some very unpleasant times. The outlets for both a husband and a wife can be so tempting. It seems easier to get needs met through fantasies or affairs. The end result, however, is heartache and destruction. What is new will someday also be old. The innocence and trust that were sacrificed for fleeting pleasure may never be restored.

Have honest discussions about what outlets are tempting. One of the things that gives pornography and attractive coworkers so much power is that they are forbidden and secret. Many men and women confess that their fantasies fade once they have shared them with their spouse. Husbands and wives should regularly ask each other, "Am I meeting your sexual needs? What temptations are strong for you, and how can I help you resist them?"

Although these conversations can be uncomfortable and
embarrassing, they can prevent tremendous heartache and
destruction. The Bible says that it is not sin to be tempted. Sin
is born when we nurture our impure desires. ". . . after desire
has conceived, it gives birth to sin; and sin, when it is full-
grown, gives birth to death" (James 1:15, NIV).

Basic Gender Differences

My first reaction to the struggles of sex in marriage was,
"Why did God have to make us so different?" It certainly
seems as if life would be a lot easier if men and women had
the same sexual appetites and preferences. But God, in His
wisdom, chose to create us with diversity. Sexual fulfillment
is the result of a journey requiring great effort, sacrifice and
communication.

Men and women differ regarding what they want out of sex.
Hart, Weber and Taylor report in their book *Secrets of Eve* that
wives say feeling close is the best part of making love. Their husbands, on the other hand, look forward to the physical pleasure
and release. This is why the health of the relationship affects a
woman's sexual desire far more than a man's. Women want sex
when they feel close, secure and rested. Men sometimes want
sex when they are tense, frustrated and stressed.

A man's cycle of arousal and orgasm is much simpler than
a woman's. He can be aroused almost immediately by an
image or thought. She, on the other hand, must focus on feeling secure, emotionally close and the physical sensation to be
aroused. It takes time and effort for her body to become ready

for sex. The slightest interference (a baby crying, pain, an offensive word he said, pressure to respond sexually) can destroy the sexual momentum that her body is building. For most women, it takes much more than straight intercourse to become sexually aroused and achieve orgasm.

Naturally, the man wants to go straight to the main course. She, on the other hand, needs preparation to even realize that she is aroused. He may become annoyed that he has to spend so much time getting her ready for sex. She is irritated that her husband never takes the time for foreplay. No wonder that sex is one of the greatest sources of stress in many marriages.

The difference that seems to cause the most trouble between husbands and wives is frequency. In most cases, men want sex more often than their wives. The average man would like to have sex about three times a week, while most women would be satisfied with once a week. Men even think about sex far more often than women. Again according to *Secrets of Eve,* men think daily about having sex, while women think about it an average of once a week.

Soon, the couple gets into a pattern in which it seems that he always wants sex from her. The wife feels as if she constantly has to meet his needs or find a way out of it. It is not long before she sees sex as a chore. He then resents her for rejecting him so often. The husband becomes desperate, for sex, and his wife feels desperate to avoid it. A mild discrepancy in frequency has now become a significant obstacle.

In 10 to 20 percent of marriages, the wife would like sex more often than her husband. This can create an even greater problem. All of her friends complain about their oversexed husbands, and she wonders, "what's wrong with me?" A woman in this situation may wonder if her husband is not interested in sex because he does not find her attractive. This can be devastating to a woman's emotional security in her marriage.

A husband's security and self-esteem can be equally affected when his wife wants more sex than he does. He may wonder whether there may be something defective about him. Why do all of his friends allude to their insatiable sex drives, while he is unable to satisfy his wife?

The Antidote

Several months ago, I read a funny quote: "Whoever said the stomach is the way to a man's heart must have failed anatomy." Accepting the fact that men and women differ sexually is an imperative first step to working through the problem. Many husbands and wives still assume that their spouse should react exactly as they do sexually.

For most men, sex is extremely important. It is the only need that they must have met by their wives. Someone else can cook their meals, clean their house, share their hobbies and listen to their problems. But no one else can satisfy them sexually without compromising their integrity.

According to Patrick Morely, the author of the bestseller *The Man in the Mirror,* sex is the number one concern of most married men. They want their wives to be more sensual, more responsive and more aggressive sexually. Lovingly handling her husband's sexuality is one of a wife's most important jobs. It may seem insignificant in the moment, but it is very symbolic of her love for him. To do this well, she must accept that he is different from her and embrace his masculinity.

Couples often come to counseling complaining that they are sexually incompatible. Of course! Most people are sexually incompatible when they begin. In fact, men and women seem by nature to be sexually incompatible. One gets aroused in ten seconds, while the other takes thirty minutes. One loves foreplay, while the other wants to go right to it. God made sex something that requires a lot of work to do well.

A basic understanding of the physical differences between men and women is imperative to working through incompatibility. Christian authors have provided a number of helpful resources. *The Gift of Sex* by Clifford and Joyce Penner and *Intended For Pleasure* by Ed and Gaye Wheat are two that I highly recommend.

Can you imagine planning dates to have sex? It may not sound very romantic, but it may revitalize your sex life. If your average sexual encounter happens out of necessity rather than desire, chances are that you need to budget both time and energy for sex.

Talking through differences and really understanding each other requires time and effort. Planning time for sex helps ensure that schedules, kids, phone calls or to-do lists will not interrupt lovemaking. Regularly block out a period of time that is set aside for physical and emotional intimacy only. Since you do not have to rush, there is ample opportunity for talking, fun and foreplay.

This strategy may also be helpful in addressing the problem of frequency. A husband, for example, may like sex three times a week. From past experience, he guesses he will be lucky if he can convince her once. If he knows that she has planned to be with him twice during the week, he feels no need to pressure her. This can relieve a great deal of tension in the sexual relationship for them both.

Emotional Gender Differences

The sexual disparity between husband and wife go beyond physiological differences. One major roadblock to understanding each other is recognizing that sex is emotionally different for husbands and wives.

Jim and Sue, although young and married only three years, rarely had sex together. Sue was like many women, and wanted to feel close to her husband, Jim, before even thinking about sex. Jim, on the other hand, believed being close *was* being sexual. He was thoroughly confused by Sue's demands to share more and feel more with her. The more she complained, the more discouraged Jim became. He had no idea how to meet her needs. Feeling helpless, he spent more time away from her, but still desired her. With even less communication, Sue was appalled that Jim expected her to please him sexually.

Jim and Sue's dilemma involved more than just sex. Jim failed to understand Sue's need for emotional closeness and intimacy in their marriage. By pulling away, he only made her feel more desperate and unlovable. Sue kept asking Jim for something that he felt inadequate to give. Every time she broached the subject, she was pouring salt in his wounds as a young, failing husband.

The Antidote

Throughout the book, we have discussed the unique needs and vulnerabilities of both a man and a woman within marriage. A woman needs to feel cherished and secure. Her husband needs to be esteemed and supported in his role as leader. These emotional needs are mirrored for men and women sexually.

The nakedness of sex leaves a woman open to her two greatest fears. The first time she disrobes in front of her lover, she is unsure whether her body will be rejected or adored. Will he focus on her beauty or on her flaws? Will her lover embrace her or reject her as she offers herself to him?

The Song of Solomon is a beautiful poetic story of two lovers marrying and consummating their marriage. The bride is known to be "most beautiful of women" (Song of Solomon 1:8, NIV). However, she expresses her fears of what her husband may find unattractive about her. In her day, beautiful women were pale. Having a tan was unattractive because it meant that you had to work in the sun. So she says to her fiancé, "Do not stare at me because I am dark, because I am darkened by the sun" (Song of Solomon 1:6, NIV).

Solomon, the groom, puts her fears to rest. He says to her what every woman wants her husband to feel about her body. After they consummate their marriage, he praises her with a whole chapter of poetry. He tells her how beautiful and fulfilling each part of her body is to him. "All beautiful you are, my darling; there is no flaw in you" (Song of Solomon 4:7, NIV). He cherishes her. She has no doubt that he is passionate about her, not another woman.

Women are also vulnerable to sexual abuse. Even within marriage, a woman's sexuality can be selfishly taken from her. A man who fondles or penetrates her without her consent and participation can easily damage her both physically and emotionally. The scars of sexual exploitation last a lifetime.

A woman's sexuality is mysteriously linked to the core of her being. It represents the most tender and vulnerable part of her. When she is sexually violated, her body, mind, emotions and even her soul feel torn apart. It is imperative that her husband protect her sexuality. His approach to her must be mindful of how fragile and vulnerable she is in their sexual relationship.

Although they act as if sex is as natural as brushing their teeth, men are also vulnerable sexually. They have emotional needs within the sexual realm that mirror what they need in marriage.

Just as men want to feel competent in marriage, they want to be good lovers. They are not so concerned about what they look like naked. But they are afraid of being ridiculed by their wives for their sexual performance. It is very important to a husband that he is a good lover and sexually pleases his wife. In fact, his sexual enjoyment will be tainted if he feels inadequate. This is why the fear of impotence is so great for a man. It is viewed as the ultimate of sexual inadequacy. In truth, most men will go through periods of impotence in their lifetime, due to a variety of factors. Husbands need their wives to affirm them sexually.

The truth is that most husbands are incompetent lovers at first. Men and women are so different sexually that a man does not naturally know how to please his wife. His instincts will likely be all wrong. This is why men need their wives' help to become great lovers. You are the only expert on your body. Your husband cannot naturally know what feels good to you, what gets you in the mood and when you are ready for the next step. He depends on you to teach him. Female sexuality is much more complicated than male sexuality. If he is going to love you well, you need to teach him how.

Sex Can Become Boring

I can remember when Mike and I were dating. Whenever he touched my hand or kissed me, I felt tingly all over. The temptation to have sex was tremendous. Our bodies seemed to crave it whenever we spent time together. We talked about how wonderful it would someday be to give into those desires once we married. Never in my wildest dreams did I imagine that we would have to work to keep sex exciting.

Sex can become as routine as doing the laundry. Without time, energy and a commitment to work on it, sex will get boring. Sustaining an arousing sexual relationship with the same person over the course of thirty, forty or fifty years is no simple feat. How can doing the same thing, in the same place, with the same person stay appealing? After all, even your favorite dessert would get old if you ate it every day of your life.

The Antidote

There are many ways to avoid dull sex. They all include variety. A couple can have sex at different times of day, and in different settings and positions. It is easy to fall prey to the myth that pure sex cannot be fun or arousing. God intended sex to be wonderfully exciting within the boundaries of marriage. In fact, Christians should be the experts on fully enjoying the gift of marital ecstasy. Clifford and Joyce Penner's book, *52 Ways to Have Fun, Fantastic Sex,* offers good examples of how Christians can thoroughly enjoy God's gift of sex throughout their marriage.

Selfishness

"Sex has more to do with love than romance." This is a statement that may surprise some women. A candlelight dinner, a back rub, bubble bath and classical music make a romantic scene. This is what many women think of as the perfect prelude to sex. For wives, sex and romance are usually inseparable. If he is not romancing her, than she has no interest in sex with him.

As women, it is easy to think that we take the higher road. He could have sex anywhere, any time, even in the middle of an argument—the animal! We know that sex can only be good when the relationship is right, when conflict is resolved and we feel close.

A woman's desire to be emotionally close to her husband before sex is no more righteous than his desire to see her in a negligee. Both are motivated by their own needs. This is why romance is so much different than love. Romance is what makes a woman feel cherished and valued. It has very little to do with him; it revolves around what makes her feel special.

Husbands and wives are naturally overly invested in what it takes for them to be sexually satisfied. It is easy to be sexually selfish. The wife will not give her body unless the marriage is strong and he has spent ample time romancing her. The husband wants black lace and sex on demand. Both become resentful of the pressures from the other.

The Antidote

The hallmark of a great sexual relationship is love. True love is a commitment to meeting the needs of the other person. A man is loving when he is patient. His desire is to move quickly to intercourse, but he knows his wife needs to be cuddled, talked to and praised. He wants her to feel safe with him sexually. This means he will understand that sometimes she just is not ready for sex.

Men also act lovingly by channeling their sexuality exclusively towards their wives. For many men, this takes great effort, and it should be acknowledged as a gift of love. There are so many sexual outlets that scream for a man's attention— pornography, affairs, fantasy and scantily-clad women, to name a few. Refusing to focus on other women or images sexually makes a tremendous statement about a man's love for his wife.

A wife also sacrifices to act lovingly in the sexual relationship. She must acknowledge that his needs are different than hers. After a day of caring for children and work, she drags herself up the stairs, pulls off her clothes, slips on a nightshirt and falls into bed, exhausted. Her husband happened to get a glimpse of flesh as she undressed and makes sexual advances toward her. This is the last thing in the world that she wants right now! She is exhausted, feels very unsexy and has not had a meaningful conversation with him in a week. Love requires that she acknowledge his need, even though she does not feel like doing so. She may need his help to get in the mood, but her willingness to fulfill him sexually is a great statement of her love for him.

I Corinthians 7:3–6 (NIV) has this to say about the sacrifice called for in the sexual relationship: "The husband should fulfill his marital duty to his wife, and likewise the wife to her husband. The wife's body does not belong to her alone, but also to her husband. In the same way, the husband's body does not belong to him alone, but also to his wife."

Over a lifetime, a great sexual relationship can only be maintained if both people are committed to loving each other sexually. God has made it practically impossible to be sexually fulfilled over time without giving to your lover. A husband will only feel sexually competent when he lovingly understands and meets his wife's needs. A wife can only feel cherished and safe in their relationship when she is sexually available and encouraging to her husband. Unselfish love, not romance, is the key ingredient.

Physical Problems

Having sex is a complex physical process that requires the cooperation of several major systems in the body. The nervous system, reproductive system, circulatory system and excretory system represent aspects of physiology that are involved in the sexual process. Hundreds of physical problems can compromise sexual performance.

Illness can be a major roadblock. Chronic pain, low thyroid, obesity and high blood pressure are just a few common conditions that can cause problems. Mental illness such as anxiety disorders or depression can also have a profound effect in the bedroom. Chronic or terminal diseases such as cancer, multiple sclerosis, and Parkinson's disease are debilitating to all physical activity, including intercourse. As if illness were not enough to destroy the mood, many medications taken for medical problems interfere with sexual desire, performance or enjoyment.

Everyday wear and tear on the body also affects sexual activity. The greatest problem for women sexually, according to a study by Archibald Hart as reported in *Secrets of Eve,* is fatigue. Forty-five percent of women, in a sample of 2,000, reported fatigue as a significant interference to their sex lives. They simply lack the energy to invest in sex.

For women, hormonal changes are often strong determinants of their sexual desire or lack thereof. Many hormonal changes occur within women throughout the month and throughout the female life cycle. Sexual appetites often wax and wane as levels of testosterone and estrogen change. Menopause, PMS and pregnancy are the most common hormonal factors that interfere with sexual desire and enjoyment. Cramps, a lack of vaginal lubrication, bulging bellies and ovulation are all examples of how hormones wreak havoc with sex.

In addition to all the other physical problems that cause "headaches," some people have "plumbing problems."

Physical ailments directly related to the reproductive organs can be responsible for prohibiting erections in men, pain during intercourse or inability to achieve orgasm. Some women experience frequent vaginal or bladder infections that regularly put a damper on sex.

The Antidote

People often endure sexual problems, never understanding that the origin might be an underlying physical condition. For example, a man can take medication for his high blood pressure for years without linking side effects to sexual dysfunction. The first step to solving a physical problem is diagnosing it. Many physical problems can be treated by a physician, but most are never even discussed with medical experts. People are, understandably, hesitant to talk to their family doctor or even a gynecologist about sexual problems.

Getting past the embarrassment and social stigma of talking about impotence, painful intercourse or a lack of sexual desire is an unavoidable step to getting help. Fortunately, most physical problems that interfere with sex can be successfully resolved with the right medical intervention.

Like any other complex physical function, sex requires two healthy, rested bodies. A commitment to health and rest is difficult to make when time is precious and life is busy. It seems easier to spend an hour grooming in the morning than spending the same hour sleeping, cooking healthy meals or exercising. Taking sex seriously means taking rest and health seriously.

Is There Ever a Time to Say "No?"

This is a very difficult question to address, yet a very real issue for some women. Kim's marriage is failing, yet her husband still wants and expects sex. Because he does not invest at all in their relationship, she feels as if she is simply a piece of meat to satisfy his physical lust. Should she participate in this?

Sex can easily be used as a weapon or manipulation for a woman to get what she wants. She can withhold sex if she is unhappy about something her husband has done or said. This is a very dangerous way to use sex. In fact, scripture tells husbands and wives not to withhold from each other sexually unless they are doing so for a time to pray and fast (I Corinthians 7:5).

In chapter four, we discussed scenarios in which a marriage becomes destructive. For example, a husband may be using his leadership in a way that is abusive or degrading to others. The relationship may also be compromised by sexual infidelity. In such marriages, a separation is necessary as a consequence of harmful behavior and to restore the marriage. To stay and "pretend" to be married may actually be enabling a pattern of behavior that is destructive and ungodly. In such cases, I believe that a wife is justified to abstain sexually.

So, what should a woman do when her marriage lacks intimacy but does not require separation? A woman should remember that the sexual relationship can be an important way of keeping her husband invested in intimacy. Although she should be sexually available to him, she should do so in the context of promoting intimacy and communication. Again, sexual intimacy should never be simply physical oneness, but emotional as well. Rather than exclusively responding physically, she may use his sexual advances as an opportunity to encourage communication and healing.

The sexual relationship is clearly a powerful force in a marriage. It can either bring the couple closer together or push them further apart. It is rife with the strongest emotions that humans can experience. Therefore, it begs to be handled with great care, sensitivity and wisdom.

Vibrant and fulfilling physical intimacy is a key ingredient of supporting and encouraging your husband. As frustrating as it may be, remember that marital sex is a powerful gift from God. Use it wisely, with love and with the intention of building oneness in your marriage.

The wise woman builds her house, but with her own hands the foolish one tears hers down.

Proverbs 14:1, NIV

Questions for Discussion and Reflection

1. Read I Corinthians 7:3–6. What do these verses mean? What implications do they have for your sex life?

2. What are the roadblocks that interfere with physical intimacy in your marriage? What steps can you take to address them?

   • Emotional

   • Relational

   • Differences

   • Physical

3. What misconceptions about sex did you grow up with? How has your knowledge of God changed your view of your sexuality?

4. Reread the section in this chapter about boundaries. Then, draw both boundary number one and boundary number two as they exist in your marriage. How can you strengthen the first boundary and relax the second?

5. How might you convince someone that sex is a gift from God? (Refer to Genesis 1:26–27 and 2:25; Isaiah 62:5; Ephesians 5:3; and Song of Solomon 3:1, 5:10–16 and 7:1–22.)

6. What can you do to be more loving sexually? (Ask your husband to help you with this question.)

Twelve

Who's Building
Your House?

*O*n the verge of divorce, Stephanie entered counseling hoping to find some reason to stay in her marriage. "I just want to be in love with my husband. Is that too much to ask?" she exclaimed. After fourteen years of ups and downs, she was fed up with her self-absorbed, fickle husband. Although Todd was not abusive nor unfaithful, he did not make an effort to meet Stephanie's emotional needs. His work, hobbies and friends seemed more important to him than his wife.

Stephanie had attempted many of my suggestions to jumpstart her marriage. She encouraged Todd and tried to understand his emotional needs. She pled with him to invest in their marriage. She examined her own attitudes and how they affected Todd. After about ten sessions, Stephanie despondently announced that her case was hopeless. "I don't think there is much you can do for me. I will just have to wait it out until I can't take any more from him."

The end of hope. What a terrible place to be!

Perhaps you have read this book and even experimented with some of the suggestions to find the hero in your husband. Maybe, like Stephanie, you are discouraged, knowing that your best attempts have failed to make a difference. If you were desperate when you read chapter one, you may now be downright convinced that nothing can alleviate your misery.

Restoring a marriage is not always about trying harder, being enlightened or waiting out the tough times. There are some cases that seem hopeless, regardless of good intentions. A wife's vows to her husband, and his to her, can be literally impossible to keep without a spiritual perspective.

Throughout this book, the central theme has been Proverbs 14:1. Each chapter has concluded with the thought, "The wise woman builds her house, but with her own hands the foolish one tears hers down." Wisdom and effort are essential ingredients to building a solid marriage. However, they alone are often insufficient. A wife can go a long way to provide an environment that allows for an intimate relationship. However, she cannot make it happen.

"Unless the Lord builds the house, they labor in vain who build it. . . . It is vain for you to rise up early, to retire late, to eat the bread of painful labors; for he gives to his beloved even in his sleep" (Psalm 127:1–2, NASV). Wow! It is only the Lord who can ultimately build Stephanie's house. Without

Him, all of her labor is vain. He wants to give to her even in her sleep.

This is consistent with the many Proverbs which teach that fearing God is the very beginning of wisdom. To be a wise woman, you must recognize the importance of God in all that you do. You cannot build your house without Him. Perhaps this is why all of your efforts have felt like beating your head against a brick wall. Although you can influence your husband, you cannot ultimately change his heart.

©2001 Julie Anderson.

Why Are You in This Marriage?

Ideally, a wife's efforts to improve the marriage and to love her husband more completely will not be in vain. A husband often responds lovingly to his wife's attempts to find the hero in him. However, this is not always the case. For a variety of reasons, some men refuse to love, to trust and to give. Like Stephanie, the women married to these men are faced with a choice: do I give up or keep going?

As discussed in chapter four, some women are married to men who are abusive or sexually unfaithful. I believe scripture is clear that these are grounds for separation or divorce. In fact, a woman who endures such an ongoing relationship is inadvertently condoning this behavior. Realistically, however, this is not why most marriages break apart. The temptation to give up on a marriage because it is disappointing or unsatisfying is what overwhelms many women. This is particularly true in a culture that is so focused on self-fulfillment.

Ultimately, a woman will decide how to react to disappointment based on how she views marriage. Everyone gets married in order to get something out of it. Love, companionship and intimacy are all common expectations. But is this the only reason why people marry? Is this the purpose of marriage?

If marriage is ultimately about getting our own needs met, then marriage is over when intimacy fails. However, marriage can also be viewed as something beyond our needs. It is often the ultimate test of our values and character. Like no other relationship, marriage can highlight our fears and selfishness. It is essentially a ministry. The way we respond in marriage reflects our core beliefs and our very reason for living.

Being a faithful and loving wife ultimately relies upon our choice to be faithful to God. Especially when a husband is unlovable, continuing in the marriage is only possible when our life means more than finding pleasure, fulfillment and happiness.

History is replete with amazing stories of men and women who endured great pain and hardship for the sake of their belief in a great cause. Even today, Christians around the world sacrifice their lives for the sake of Christ. This is what God calls every Christian to be ready to do. Currently in America, we are unlikely to have to choose Christ in the face of death. Although we may not be called to die for Him, we are called to live for Him. This means putting our own desires and ambitions aside. Romans 12:1 says that we are to be living sacrifices. In Matthew 16:24–25 (NIV), Jesus said to His disciples: "If anyone would come after me, he must deny himself and take up his cross and follow me. For whoever wants to save his life will lose it, but whoever loses his life for me will find it."

You may be willing to die for Christ, but are you willing to live for Him? Are you willing to put aside your own needs and depend upon Him? This is a hard teaching. Our entire culture is built around identifying and satiating our personal needs and desires. To deny ourselves and willfully stay in a situation that is uncomfortable and unsatisfying is crazy by today's standards.

This is where building a marriage becomes impossible without a reliance upon God. As long as marriage is only for personal fulfillment, staying in such a union makes no sense. The world's answer is to move on to the next guy. However, when marriage is viewed as a calling or a ministry, hope resurfaces in the midst of broken dreams. The hope is no longer that the frog will turn into Prince Charming. There is, instead, hope that God can be glorified through what seems like a tragedy. It is only in seeking God and His plan to build the "house" that forgiveness and unconditional love can infuse life into a dead marriage.

Starting over does not mean finding a new man to be your prince. A new beginning is only possible through striving and praying to see marriage, yourself and your husband as God does. He wants to be glorified through you in your marriage: for better or worse, for richer or poorer, in sickness and in health, till death separates you. This is not a pessimistic message! It means wherever you are, God can restore and redeem you. Nothing can interfere with your faithfulness to Him except your will to resist Him.

But What About My Unmet Needs?

The disappointment that comes with marriage is relative. Some women experience great despair and pain, while others are blessed with loving, well-intentioned husbands. Regardless of how solid a marriage is, every wife has experienced disappointment, great or small. No husband can ultimately satisfy his wife's greatest needs. In the end, marriage never delivers what a bride hoped it would.

If being married is not about getting needs for intimacy and companionship met, then what is the purpose? Although

God's design is for a husband and a wife is to become one, the reality of marriage falls far short.

Marriage is a mystery that is meant to awaken and illuminate our hunger for Christ. Throughout the Bible are references describing marriage as a metaphor for Christ and His people. It is only through the marriage experience that a woman can understand her longing for a bridegroom who will love and sacrifice unconditionally. The emptiness and disappointment that surface in marriage are not supposed to signal the end of hope, but begin the need for true hope. Marriage is not meant to satisfy, but to ignite the passion for which we were created—intimacy with God.

Although God may ask you to persevere through a marriage that is disappointing and unfulfilling, your needs are important to Him. He does not ask you to ignore your longing for love and companionship, but to trust Him with them. In Matthew 6:26 (NIV), Jesus said, "Look at the birds of the air, they do not sow or reap or store away in barns, and yet your heavenly Father feeds them. Are you not much more valuable than they?"

Psalm 146:3 (NIV) says, "Do not trust in princes, in mortal men who cannot save." Even the best husband cannot provide salvation—spiritually or emotionally. No matter how good your marriage, you will go through times of drought. Your husband was never meant to completely satisfy you, nor you him.

Perhaps the most touching conversation Jesus had with a human while on earth was with the Samaritan woman recorded in John 4. This woman had been married five times and was currently living with someone to whom she was not married. She was thirsty for love. Try as she might, the affection of a man never satisfied her. She probably hoped that the next guy just might be the hero she was longing for. Jesus knew her thirst for love, just as he knows yours. He said to her: "Everyone who drinks of this water will be thirsty again, but whoever drinks the water I give him will never thirst. Indeed, the water I give him will become in him a spring of water welling up to eternal life" (John 4:13, NIV).

Is your well dry? Do you feel as if you have little to give your husband? How can you love him when he has given you nothing? The answer is Jesus. Imagine a well of love springing up inside of you. No longer are you dependent on your husband's touch or compliment to make it through the day. He, beloved, is your bridegroom. Only He is able to love you perfectly. He loves you with "an everlasting love" (Jeremiah 31:3, NIV).

None of us deserves God's love and mercy. It has nothing to do with our merit or love for Him. He simply loves us! No matter what has transpired in your past, He is on his knee, asking to be your loving husband. Encouraging godliness in your husband must begin with accepting God's love and forgiveness in your own life.

You can only invest in your marriage when your life and your happiness do not depend on the success of finding the hero in your husband. If you are desperate for a knight in shining armor, you will not be able to vanquish your insecurity and disappointment long enough to invest in a mortal husband. You must depend on God and his provision for your ultimate worth and stability. Only then can you freely obey God's wisdom rather than your fears.

Intimacy with your husband is a goal worthy of your attention and efforts. I have written this book because I truly believe in the importance of marriage. I also believe that the biblical and psychological principles presented can significantly improve trust and intimacy within marriage. However, there are many happily married people who are spiritually dead. A great marriage is a good thing, but it is not the best thing.

Please do not allow either your disappointment or your happiness in marriage to interfere with what is most important—intimacy with God. Both the excitement of a growing marriage and the despair of brokenness are chances to seek and glorify the Lord. What an inspiration the apostle Paul was in his letter to the Philippians when he wrote: "I know what it is to be in need, and I know what it is to have plenty. I have learned the secret of being content in any and every situation. . . . I can do everything through him who gives me strength" (Philippians 4:12–13, NIV).

*U*nless the Lord builds the house, they labor in vain that build it.

Psalm 127:1, NASV

Questions for Discussion and Reflection

1. Read Proverbs 14:1 and Psalm 127:1. Do these verses contradict each other? What role does a woman play and what role does God play in building a house? How might a wife's efforts get in God's way?

2. Why does Jesus repeatedly refer to himself as a "bridegroom" throughout the New Testament? In what ways is He *your* husband?

3. What is the purpose of marriage? How does the way you act in marriage reflect your character and values?

4. Describe the kind of hero you see in your husband. How can you work with God to discover those qualities in him?

5. Are you willing to invest in your husband without the guarantee of his response? Why or why not?

Bibliography

Cloud, Henry and Townsend, John. *Boundaries.* Grand Rapids: Zondervan Publishing House, 1992.

Crabb, Lawrence J. *The Marriage Builder.* Grand Rapids: Zondervan Publishing House, 1992.

Dobson, James C. *Love Must Be Tough.* Nashville: Work Publishing, 1996.

Gray, John. *Men Are From Mars, Women Are From Venus.* New York: HarperCollins Publishers, 1995.

Hart, Archibald D.; Hart, Catherine Weber; and Taylor, Debra. *The Secrets of Eve.* Nashville: Word Publishing, 1998.

Levinson, Daniel. *The Seasons of a Man's Life.* New York: Random House, 1979.

Markman, Howard J.; Stanley, Scott; and Blumberg, Susan L. *Fighting for Your Marriage.* San Francisco: Jossey-Bass Inc. Publishers, 1996.

McGee, Robert S. *The Search for Significance.* Nashville: Word Publishing, 1998.

McQuilkin, Robertson. "Living by Vows," *Christianity Today's Marriage Partnership,* Fall 1996.

Medved, Michael. *Hollywood vs. America.* New York: HarperCollins Publishers, 1993.

Medved, Michael and Diane. *Saving Childhood.* New York: HarperCollins Publishers, 1999.

Morely, Patrick. *The Man in the Mirror.* Grand Rapids: Zondervan Publishing House, 2000.

Penner, Clifford and Joyce. *52 Ways to Have Fun, Fantastic Sex.* Nashville: Word Publishing, 1994.

——————. *Restoring the Pleasure.* Nashville: Word Publishing, 1994.

——————. *The Gift of Sex.* Nashville: Word Publishing, 1994.

Wheat, Ed and Gaye. *Intended for Pleasure.* New Jersey: Fleming Revell Company, 1981.